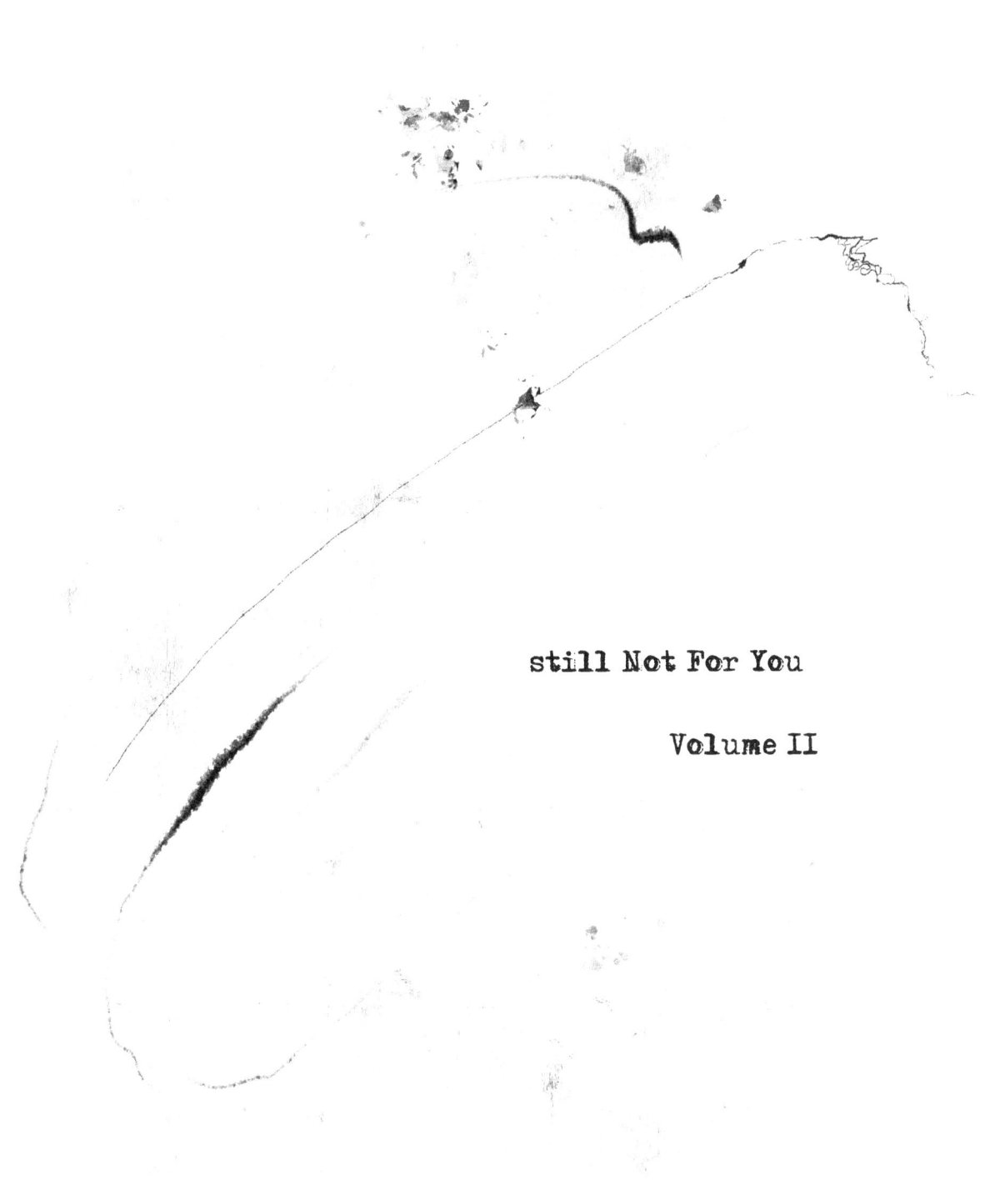

still Not For You

Volume II

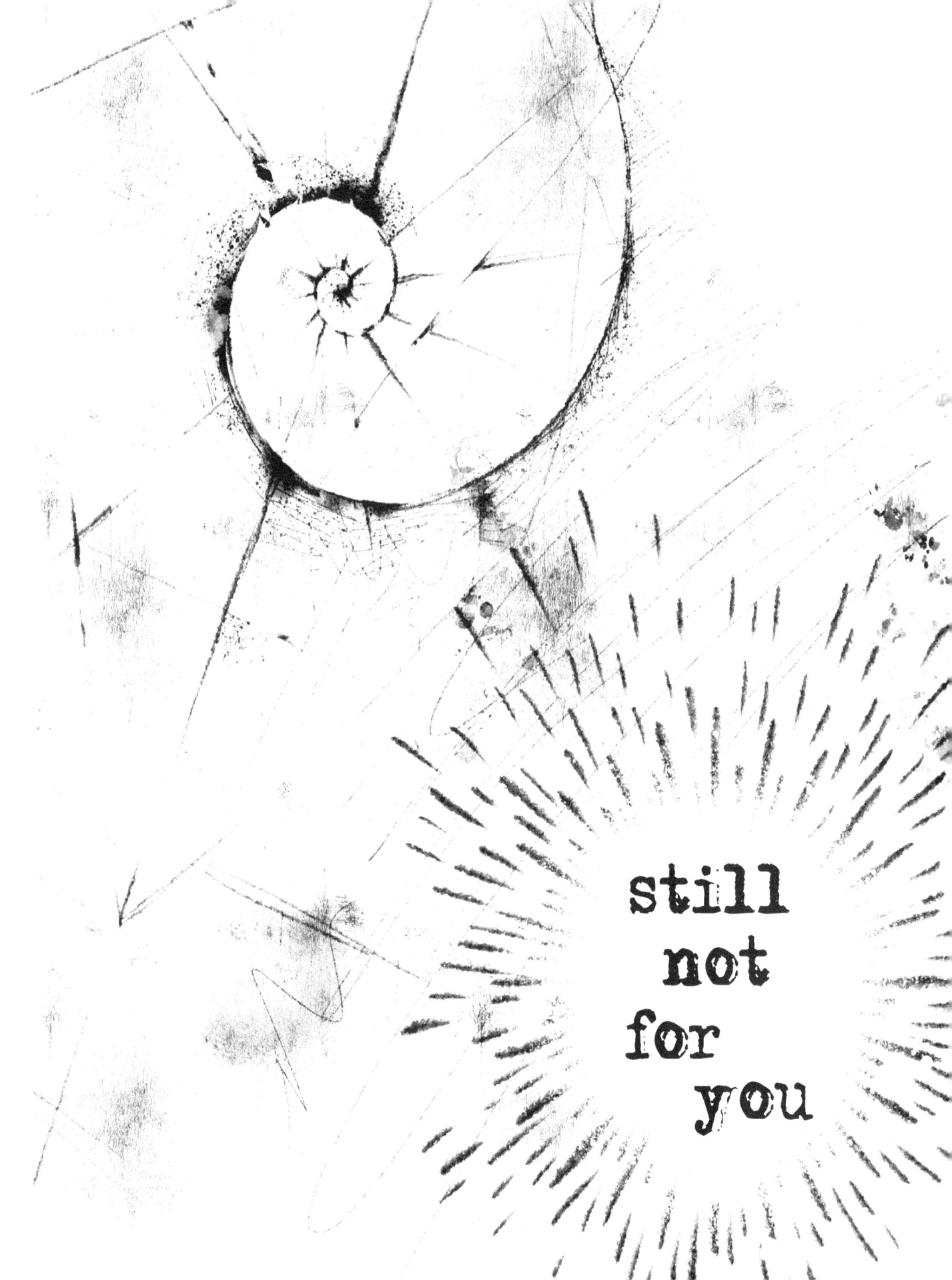

still
not
for
you

Haley's
488 South Main Street
Athol, MA 01331
800.215.8805

International Standard Book Number,
hardcover: 978-1-956055-19-1
ebook: 978-1-956055-17-7

still Not For You

Volume II

Haley's
Athol, Massachu-
setts

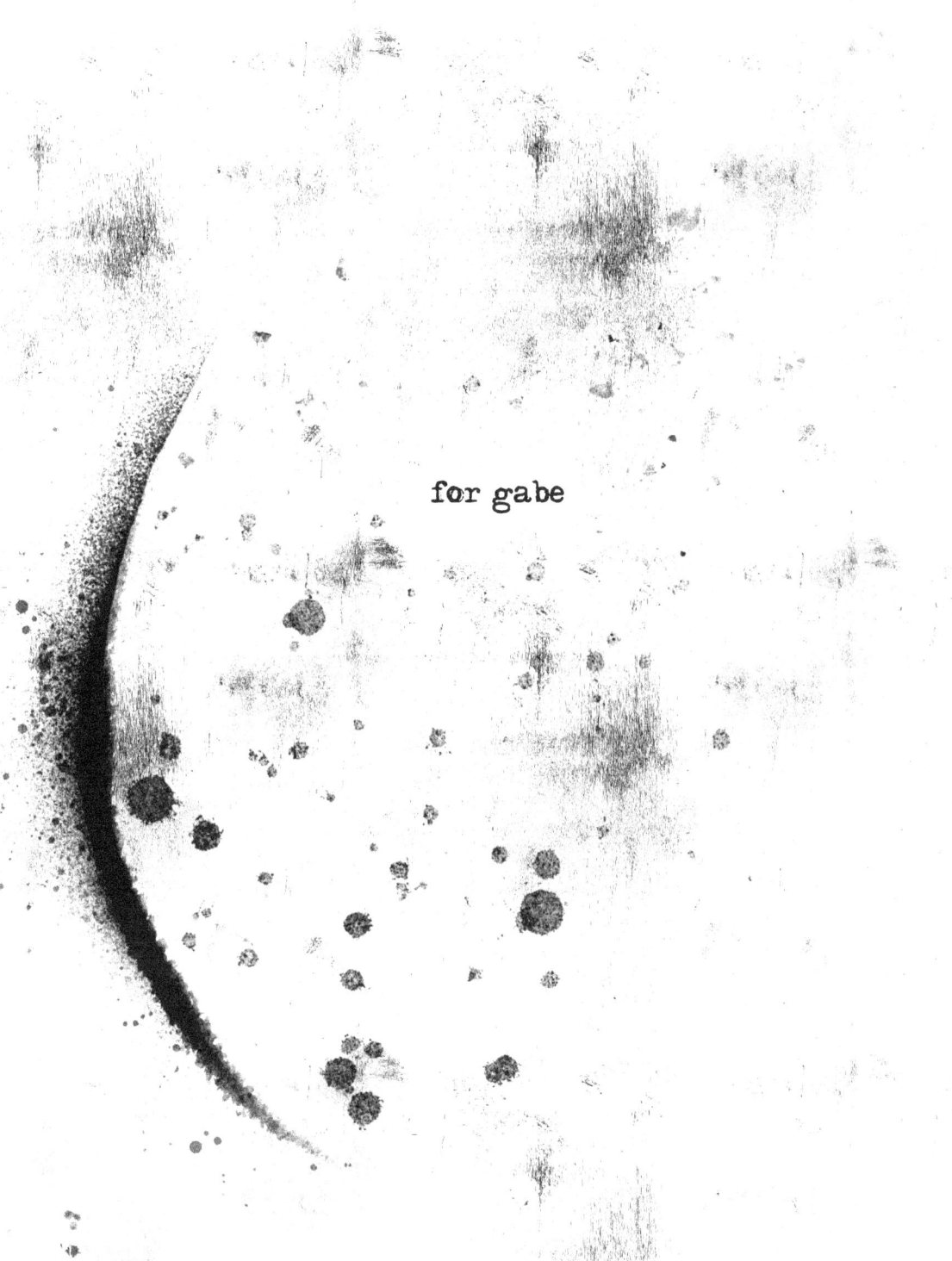

for gabe

Thanks to my parents, Red House Irons, and maybe
one or two other people. . .

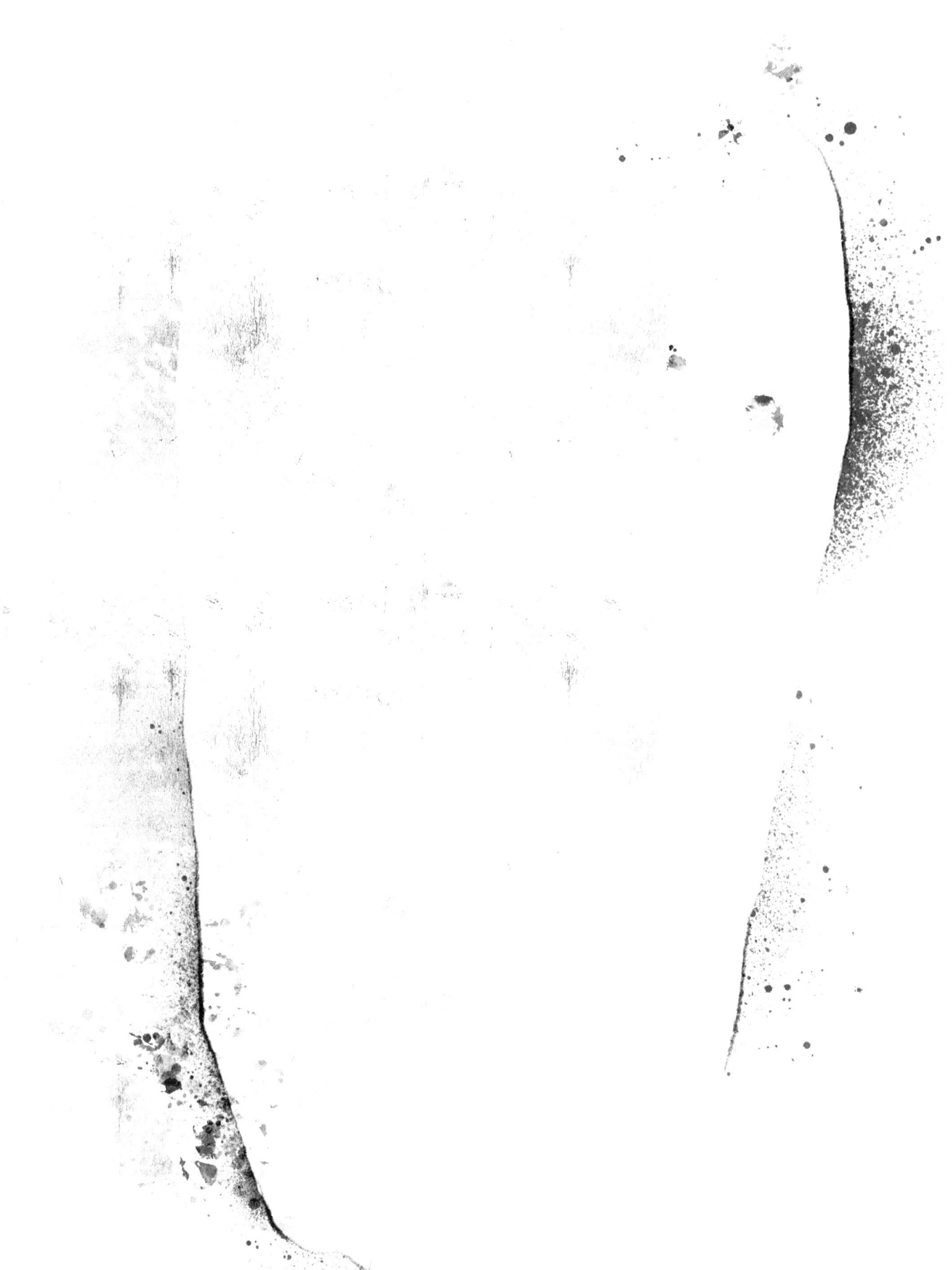

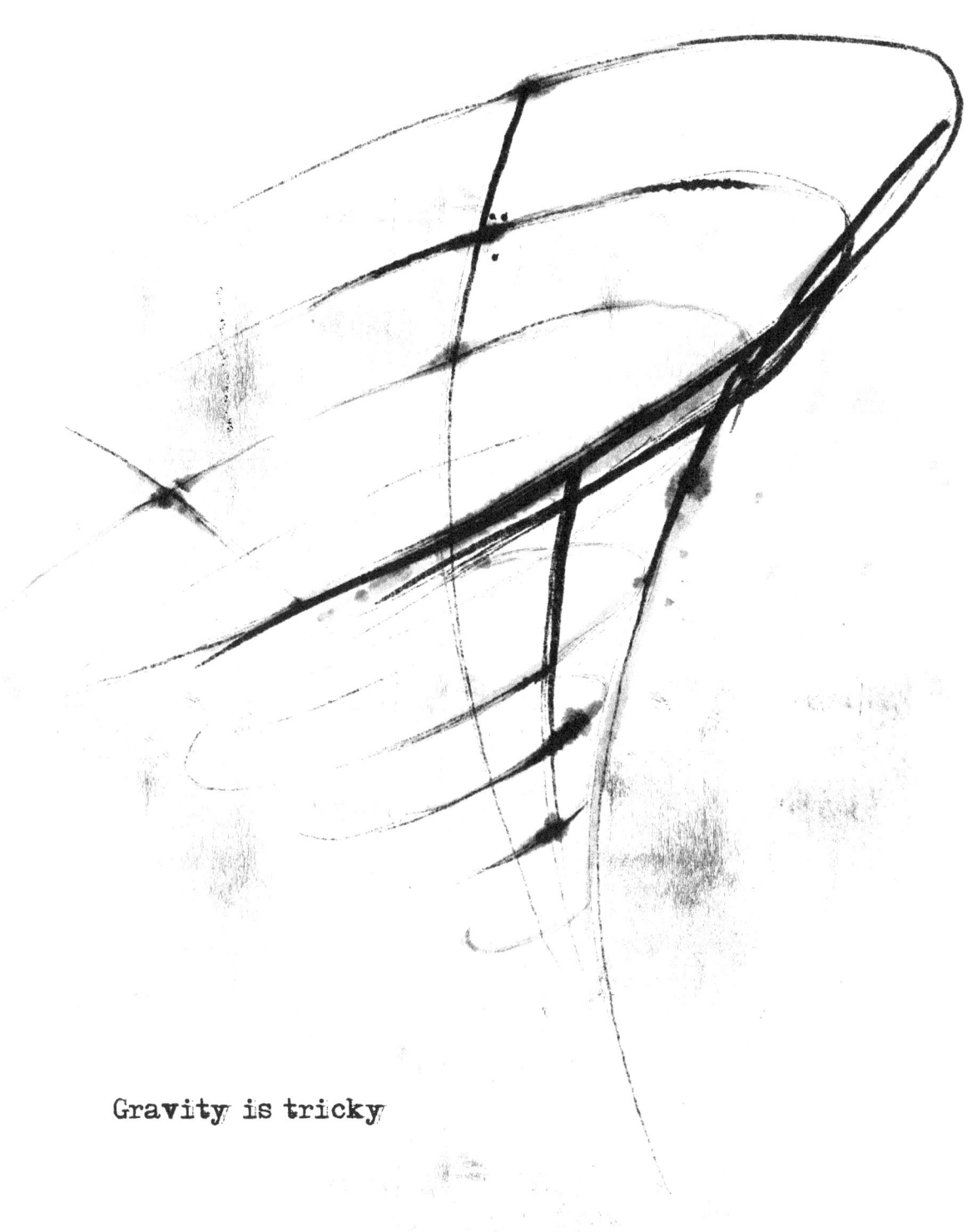

Gravity is tricky

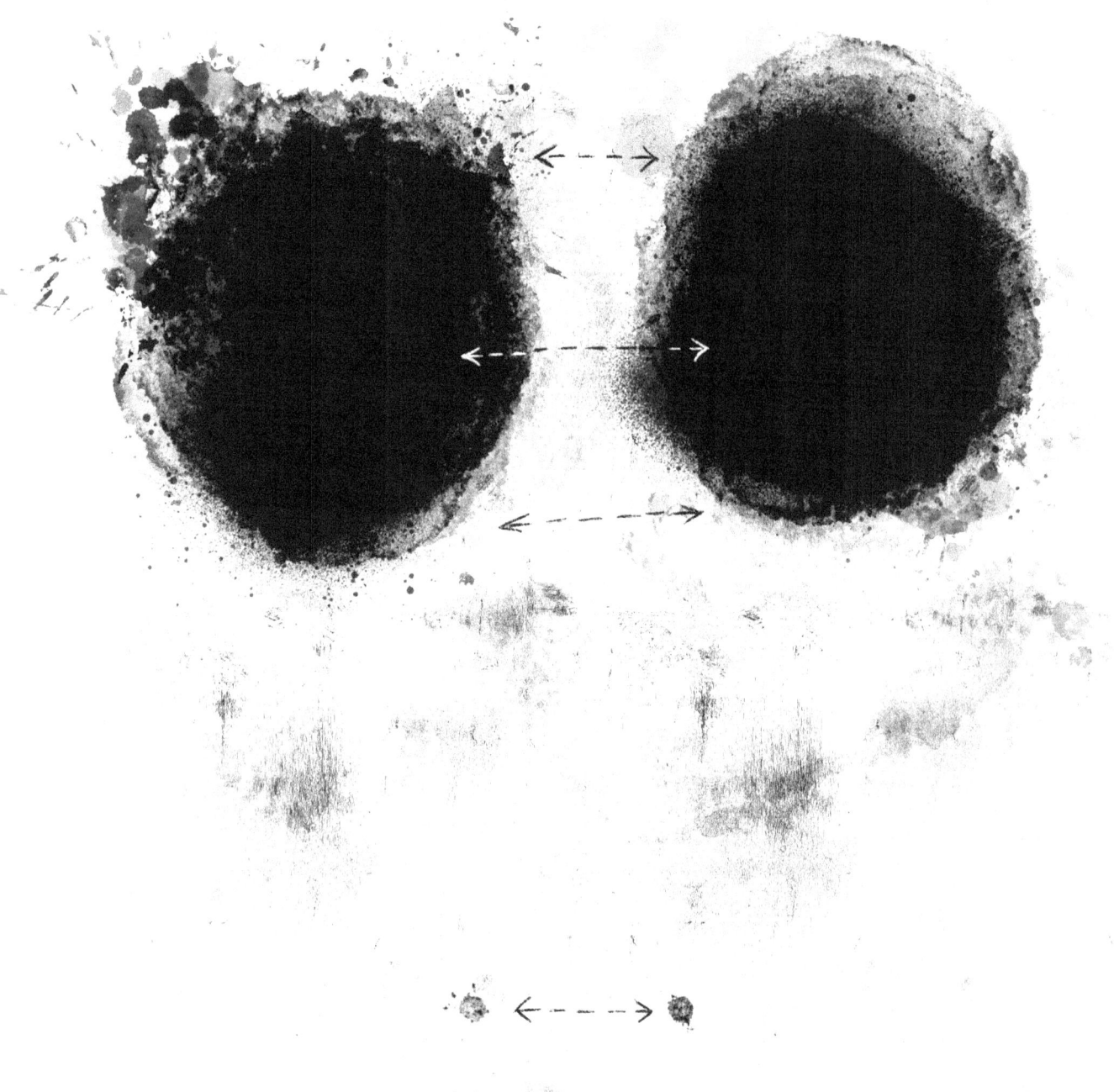

Gravity is a force of attraction

that exists between any two large masses

or tiny particles.

Gravity is a beautiful metaphor for all the things
we encounter
and

grounds our adventures

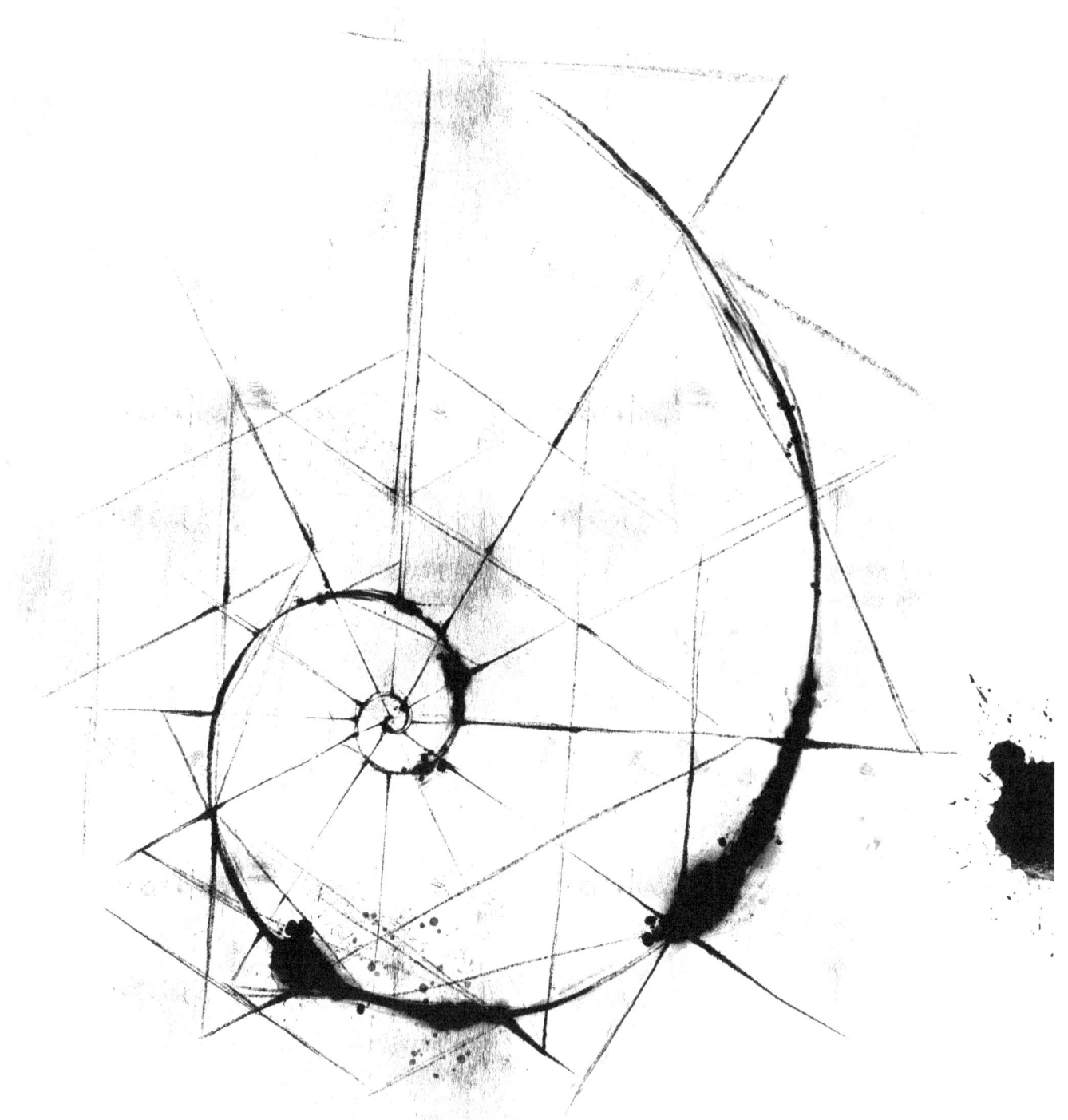

Like the changing of seasons, contrast gives rise to challenges
of conflict and harmony
Such inspiring elements that fill us with sparkling wonderment
will at some point tarnish and diminish in our eyes.

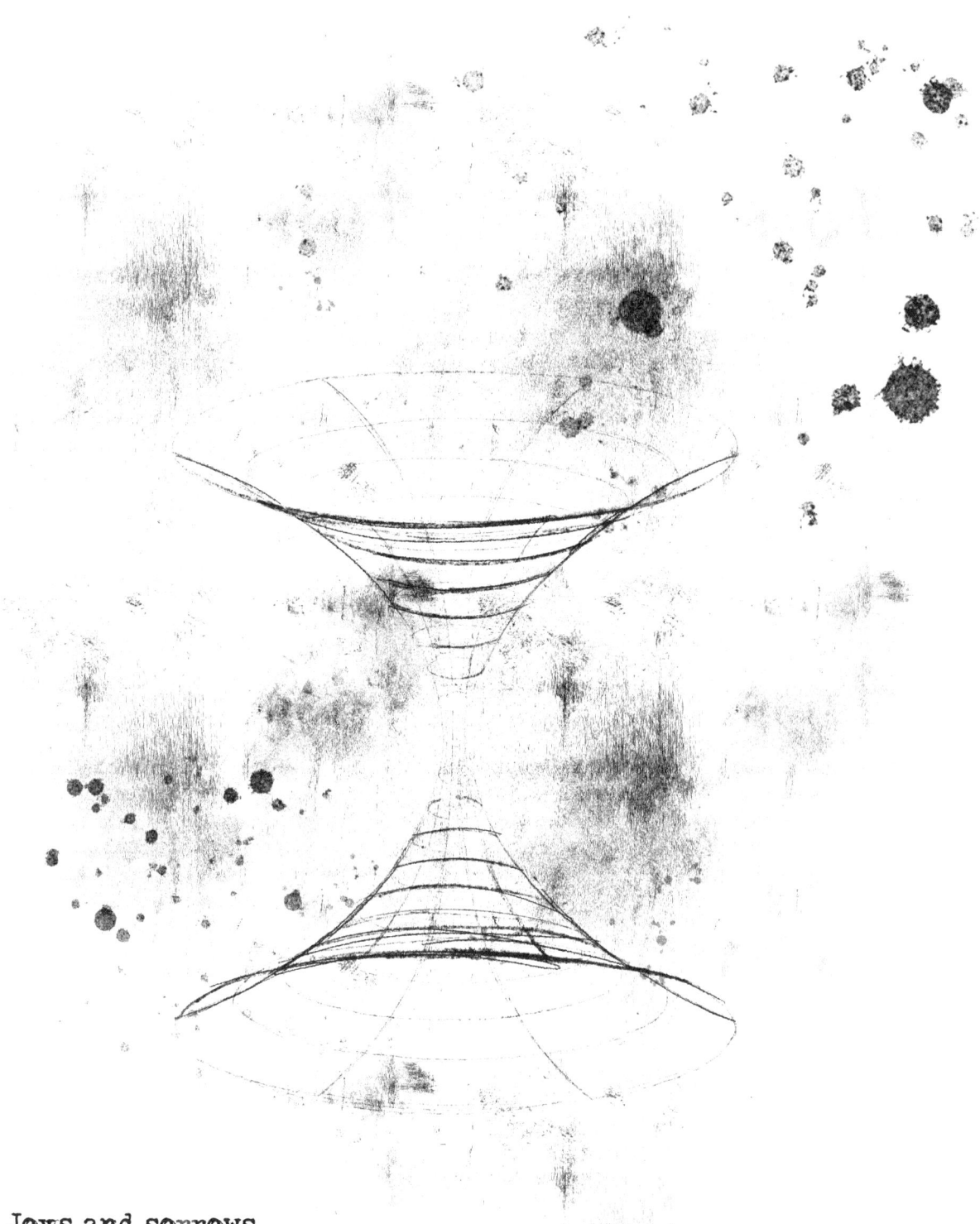

Joys and sorrows,

peaks and valleys

are all part of the physical adventure

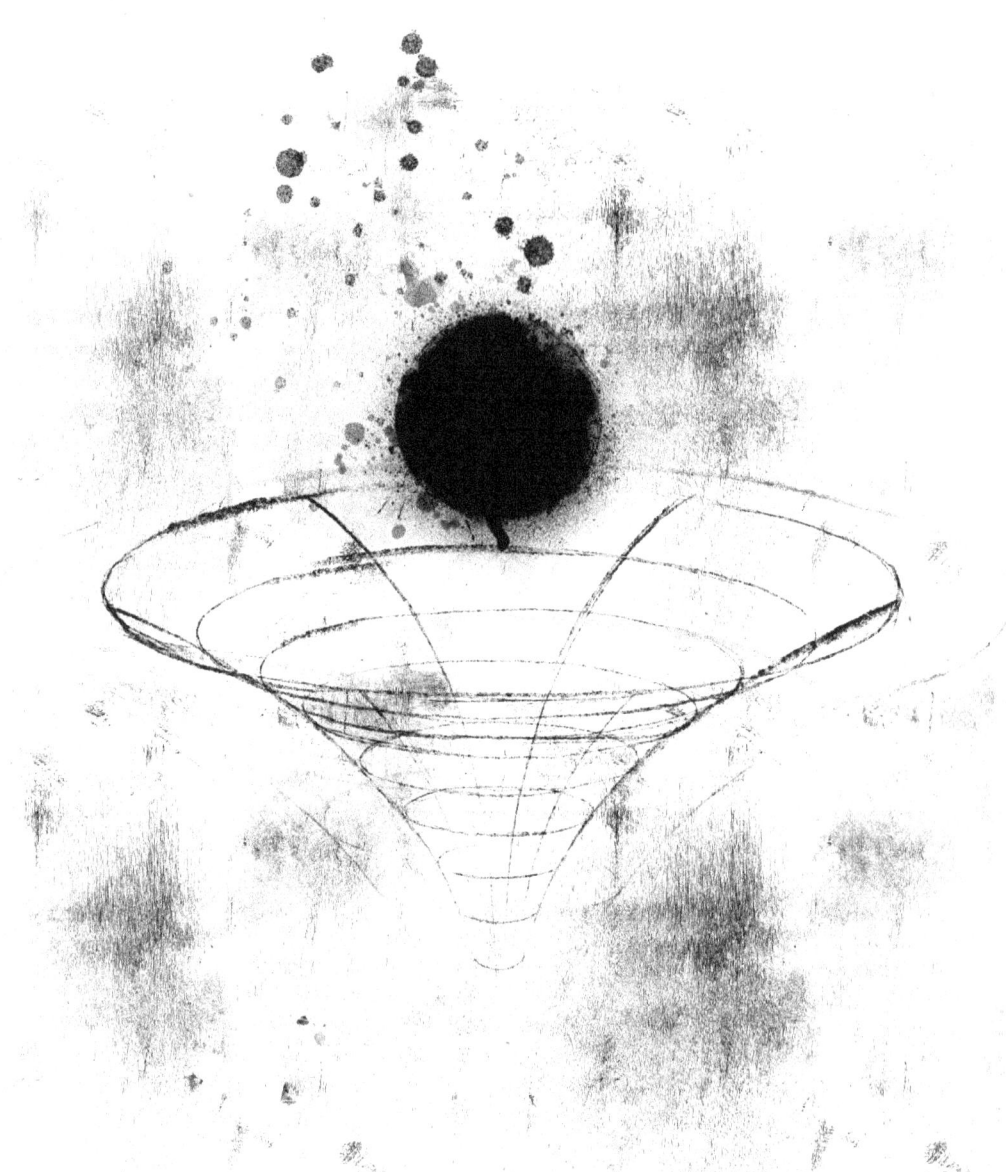

So, for as long as we can, we embrace the joys and wonderment
as they continue to inspire.

It's important to be reminded that
gravity pulls masses and particles
closer and closer to what we love.

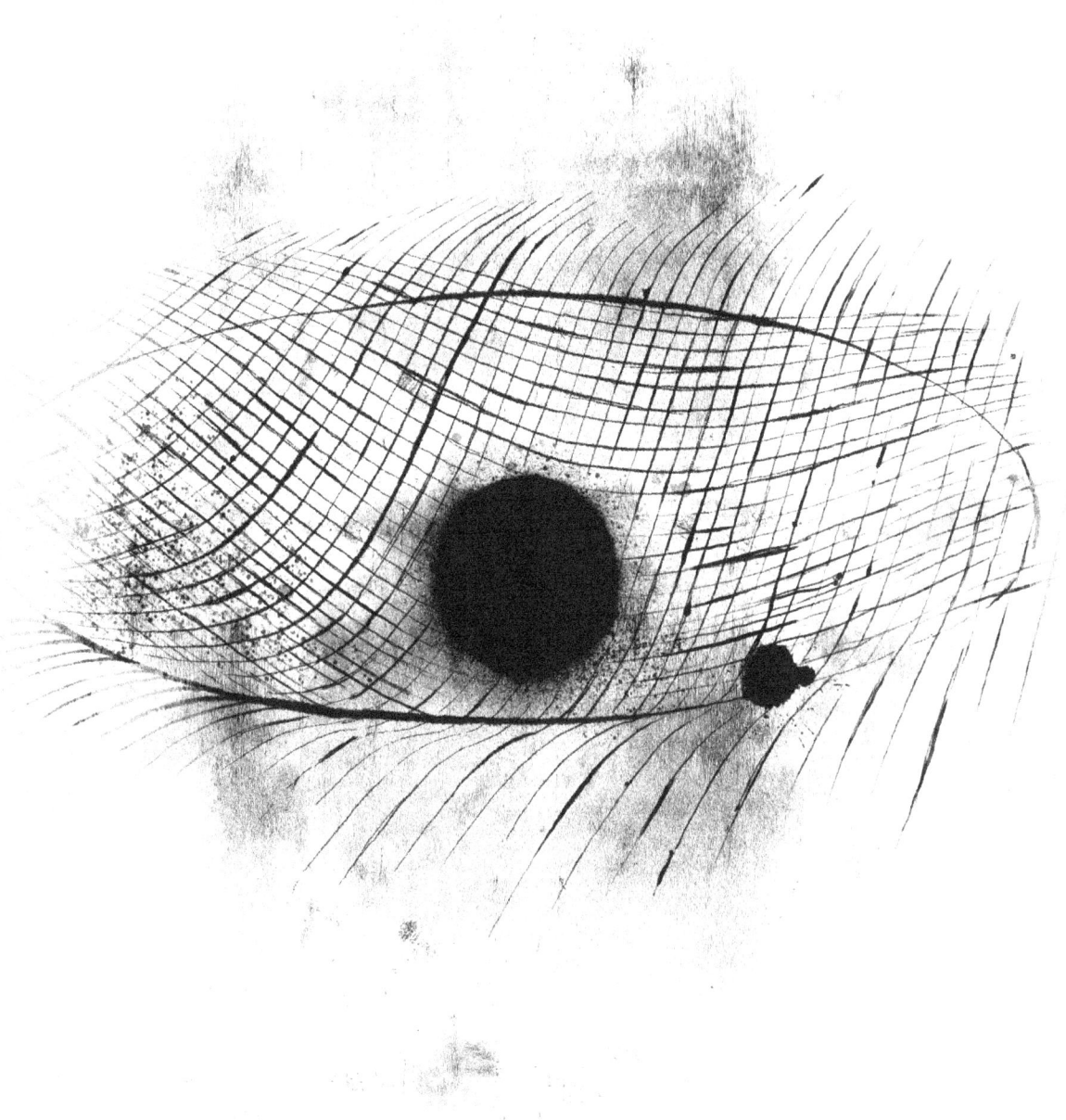

Because... Gravity   is   very   attractive.

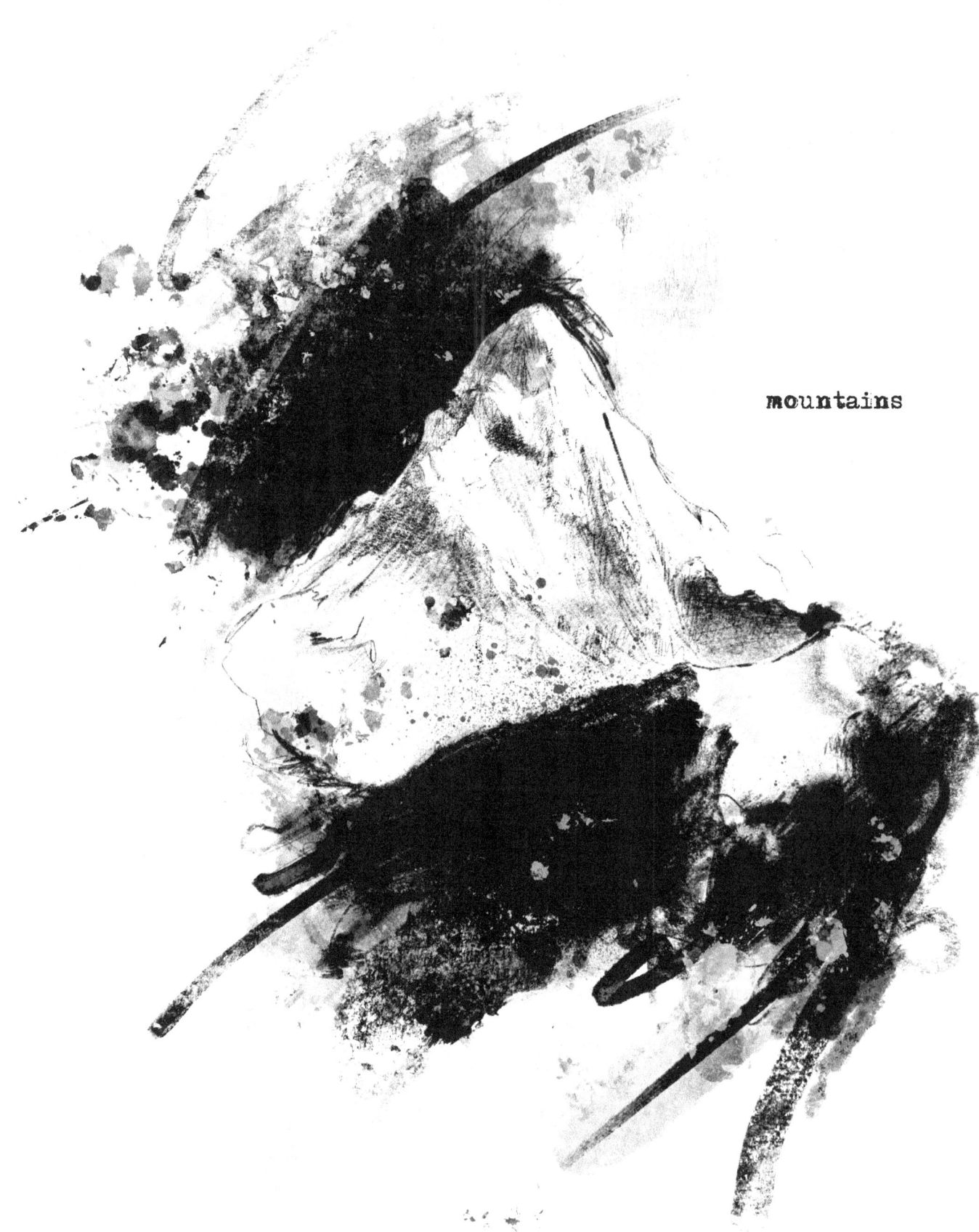

mountains

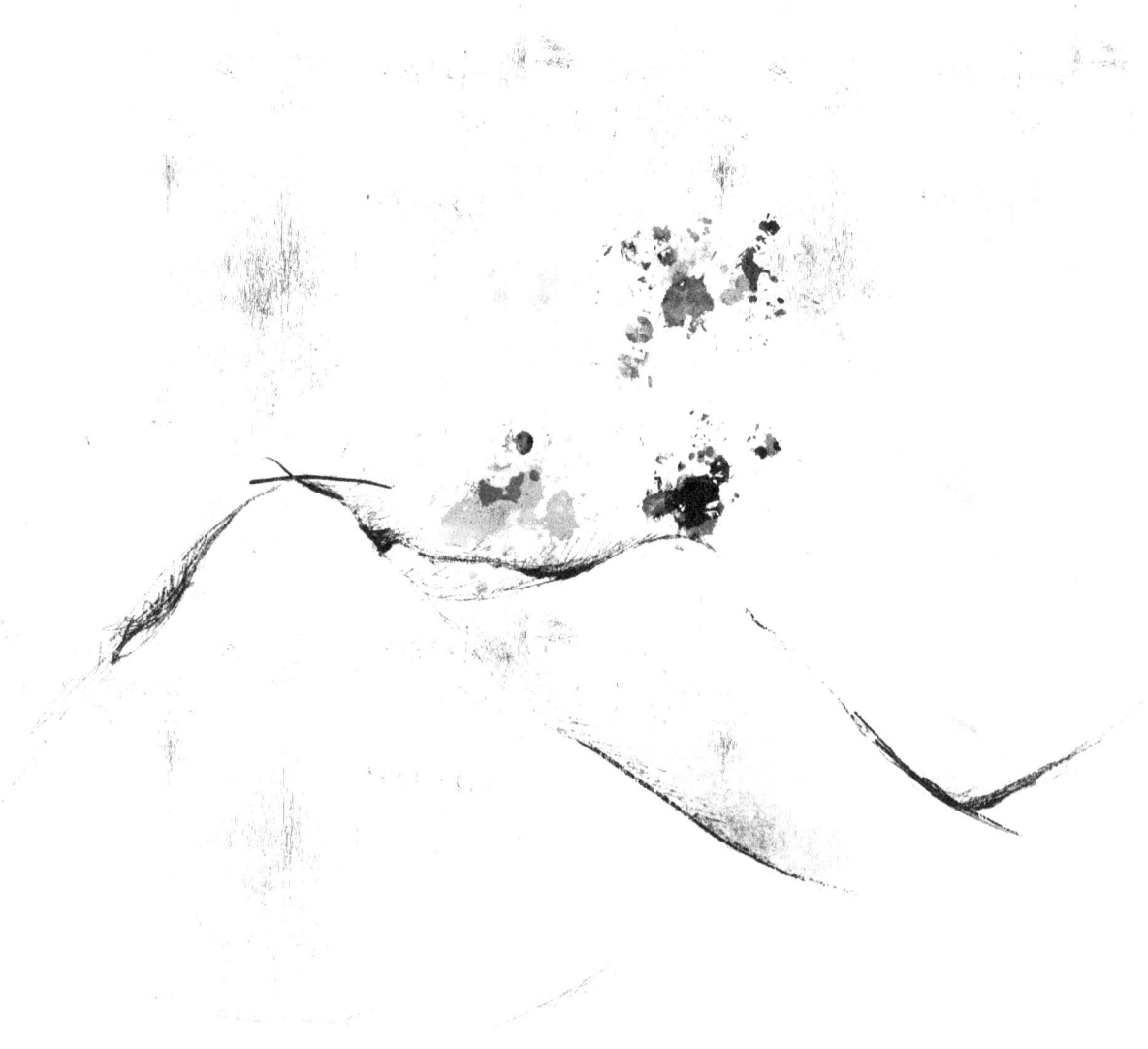

Mountains are majestic and
full of adventures.

They are old and great opportunities to see   the history
of our earth.

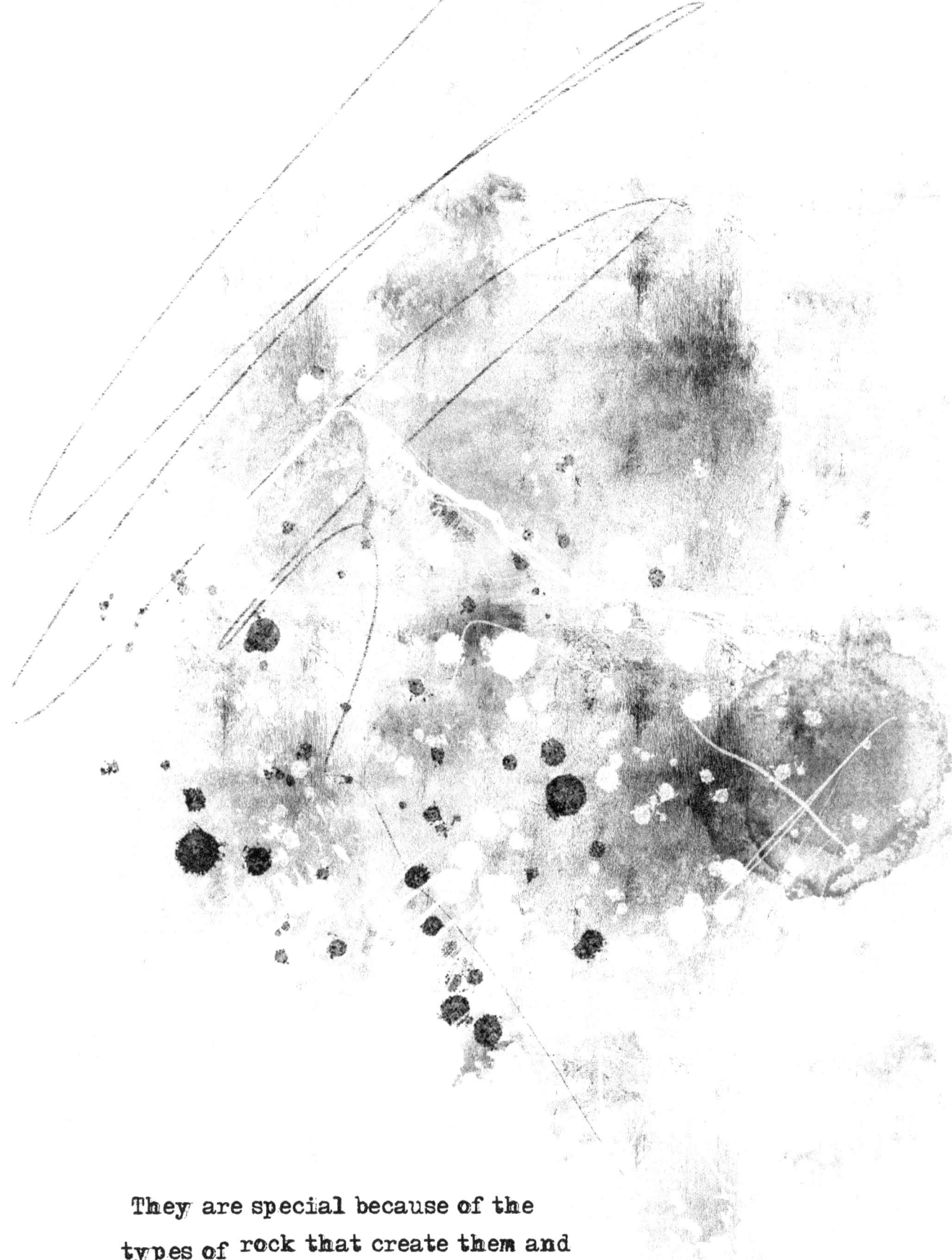

They are special because of the
types of rock that create them and
all life that adorns them

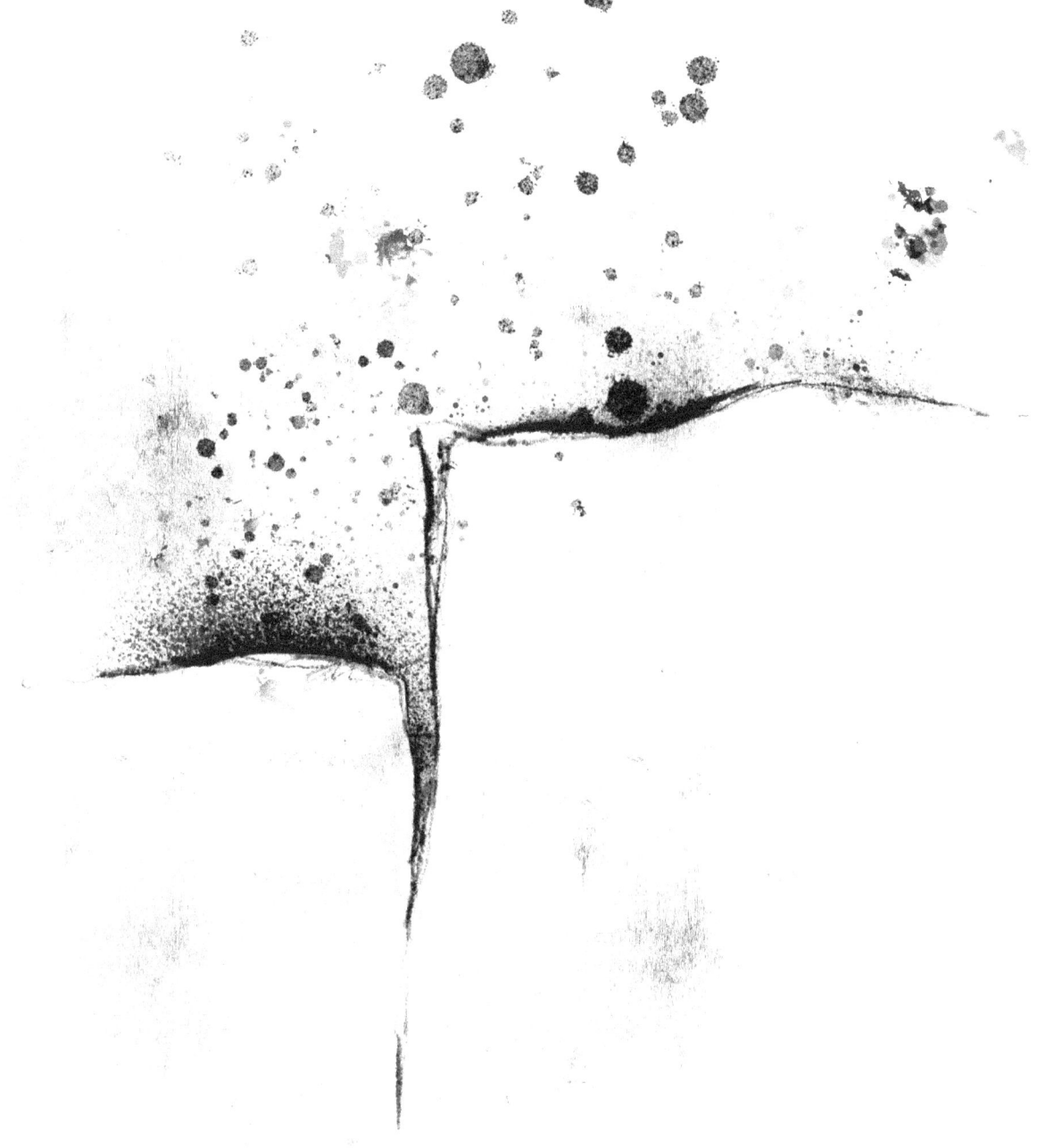

Tectonic action creates mountains.

Tectonic plates are gigantic
pieces in the uppermost mantle
of the Earth's crust

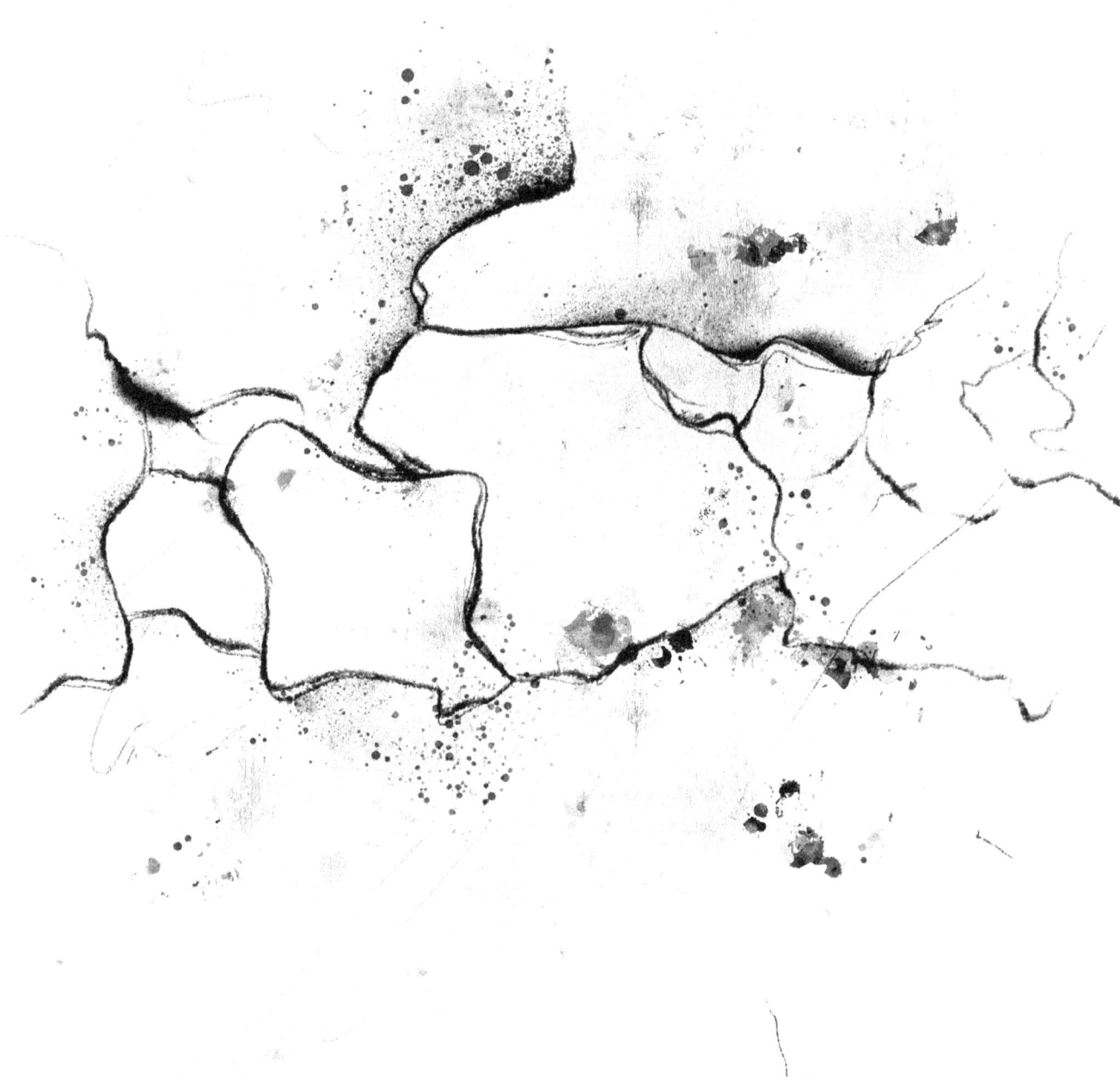

There are seven major tectonic plates —

Pacific
North American
Eurasian
African
Antarctic
Indo-Australian
South American

— and they move very slowly
but are always in motion.

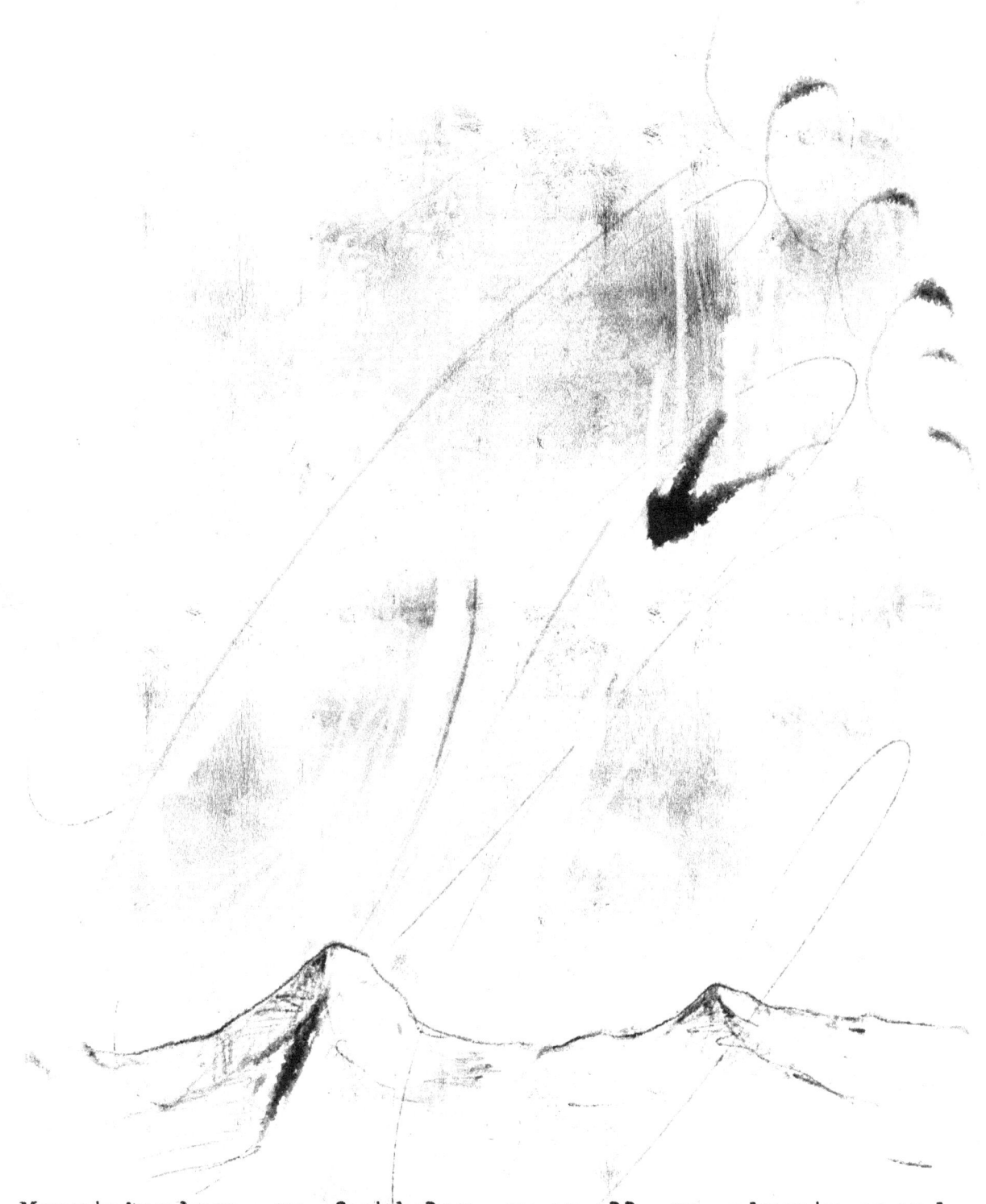

Mountains keep your feet below you on all your adventures and
challenge your mind with their dynamic ecosystems
and playgrounds of shapes
and
sizes.

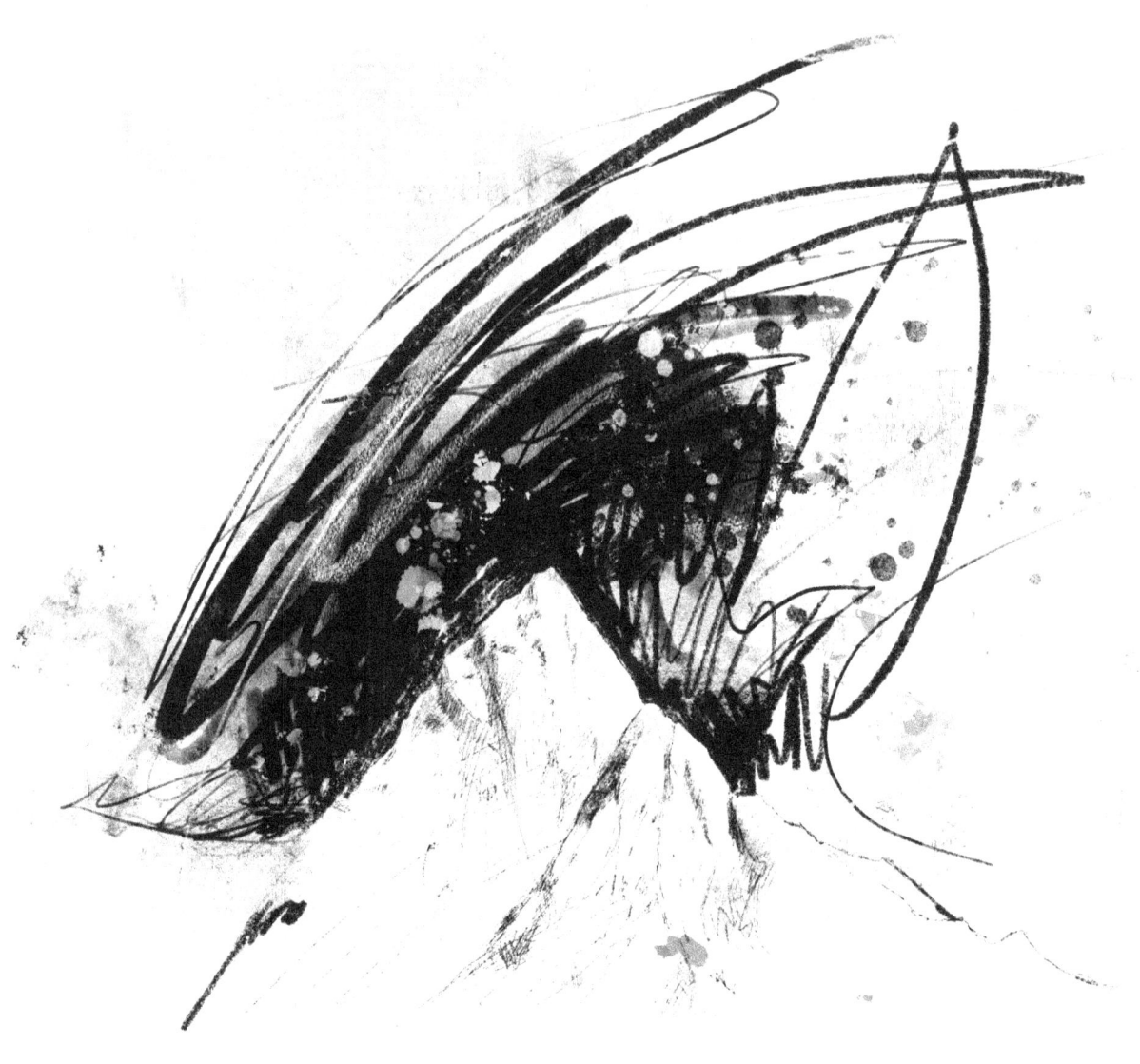

Mountains are always changing but   so slowly.

All Mountains are part of the earth and in constant change.

They are not changing for you, my love.

That is just erosion.

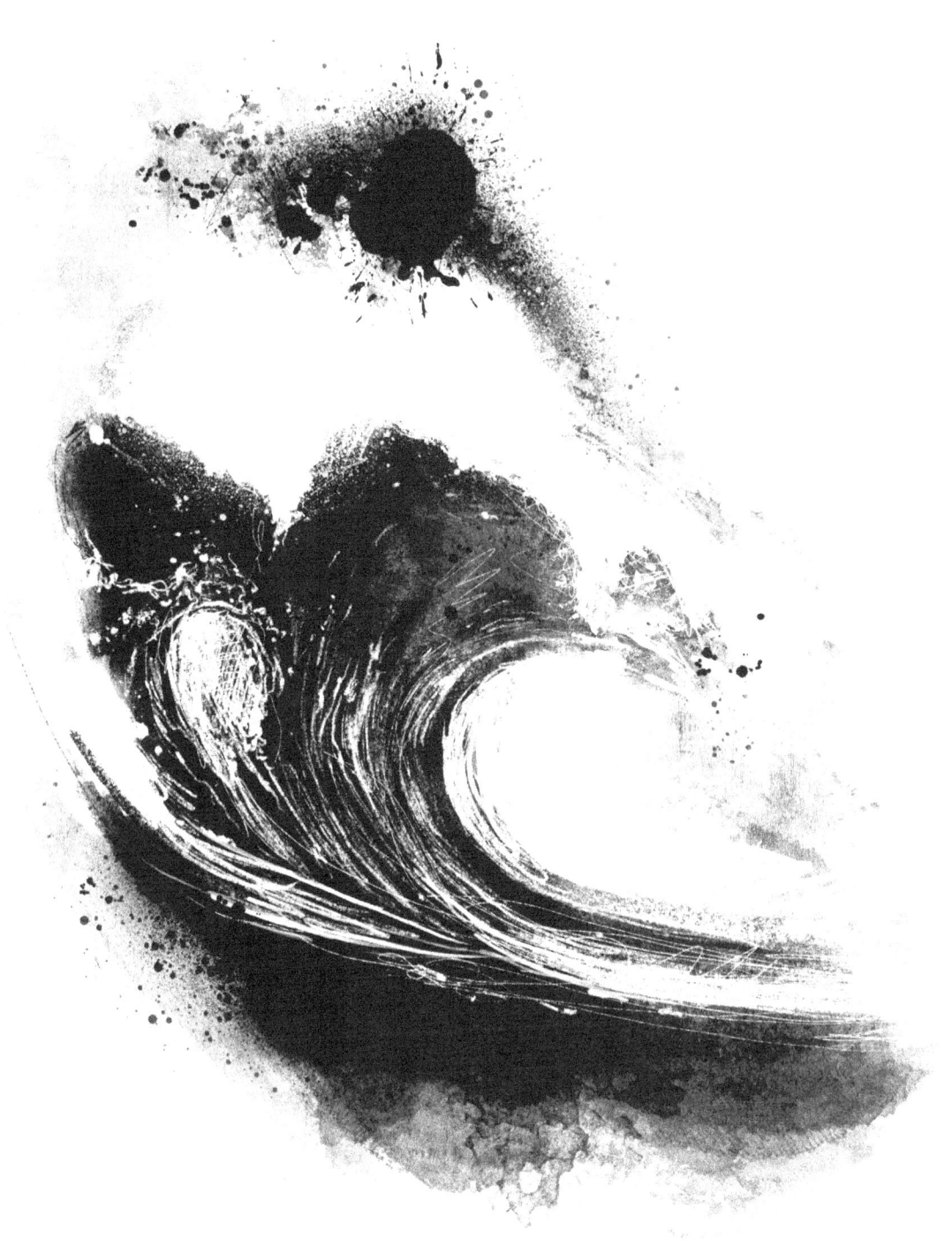

The ocean is a huge body of saltwater
that covers almost 71% of the
earth's surface.

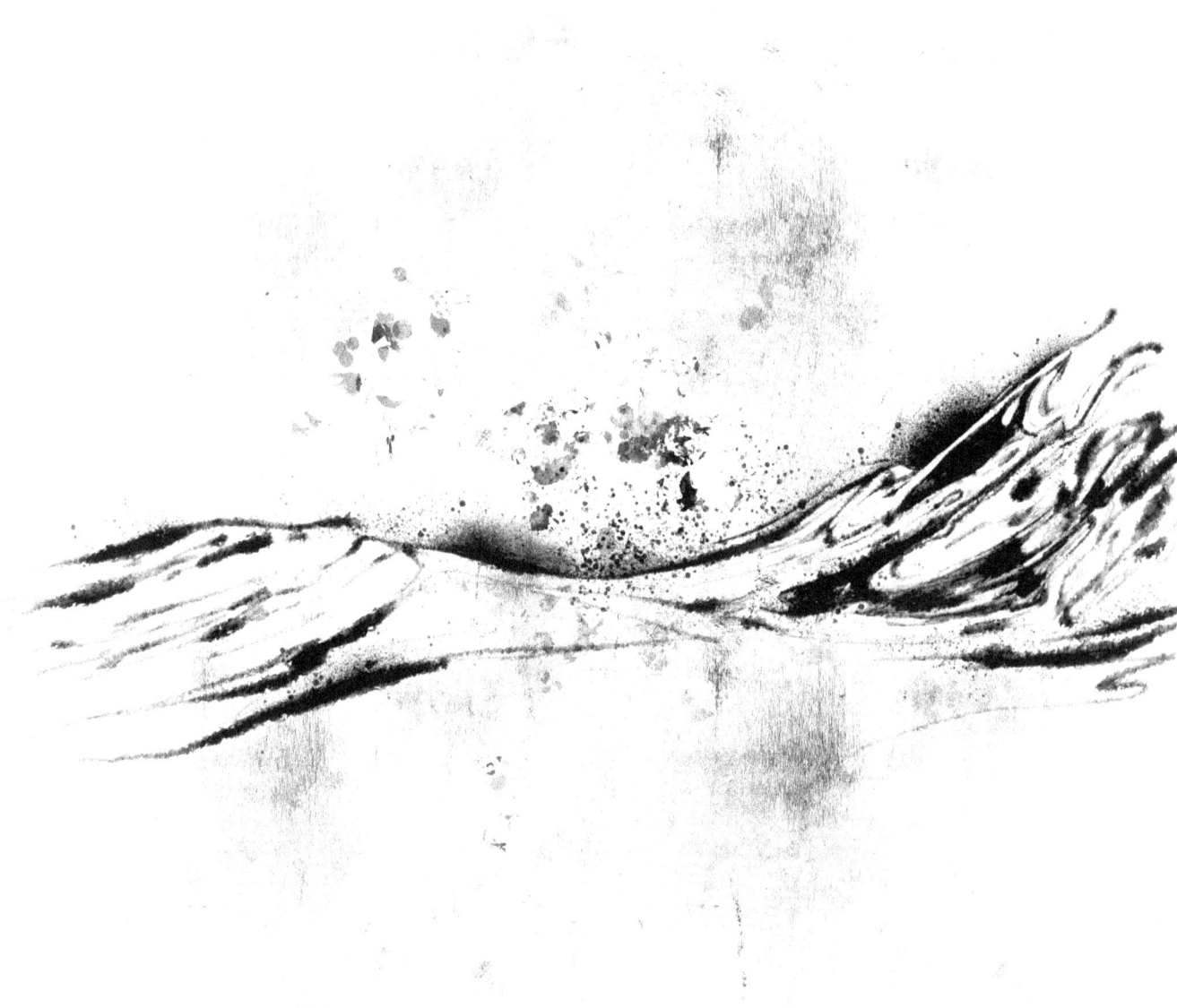

There is **only one ocean** that all the water flows freely between.

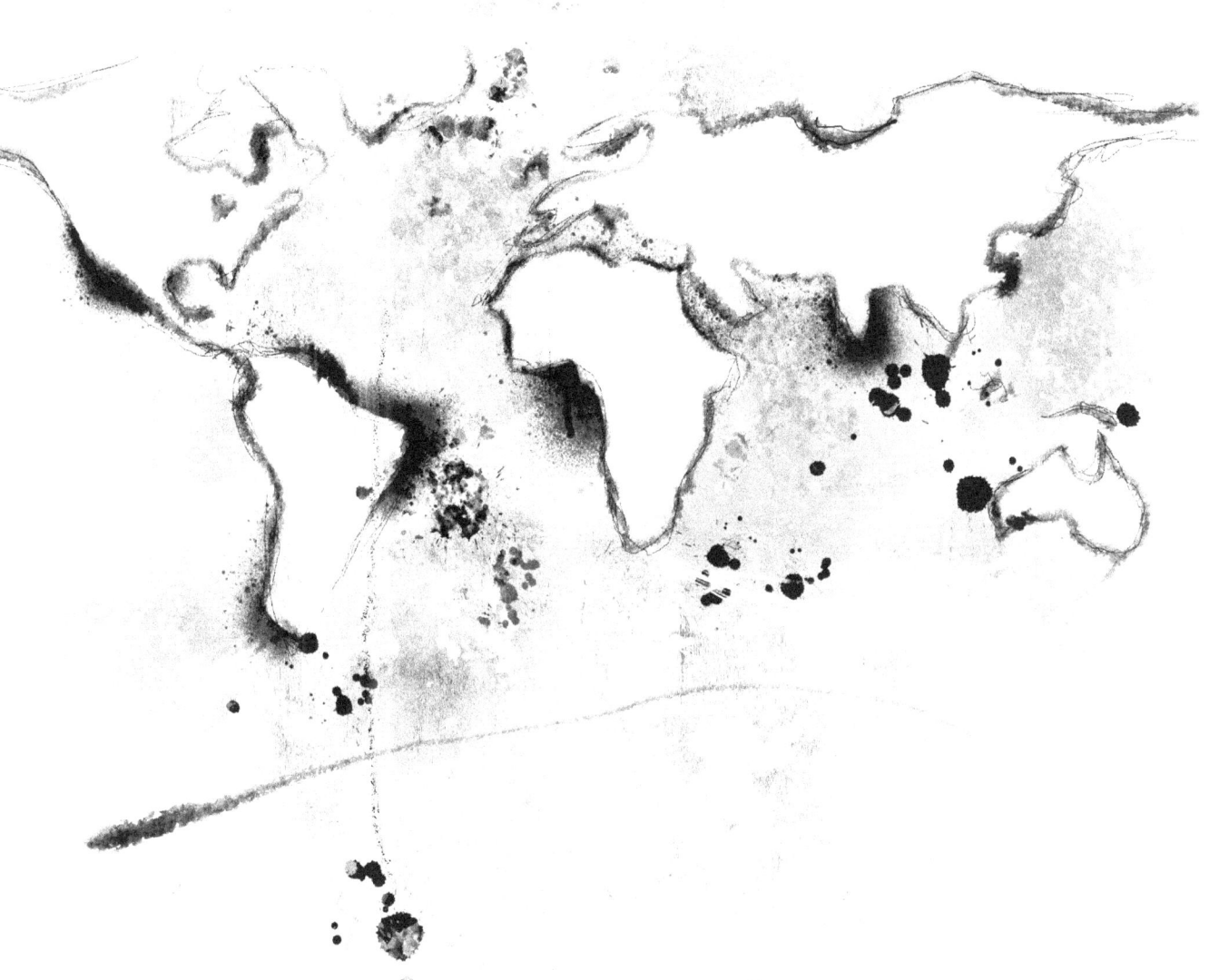

But for some reason, we like to break it up into
five sections to keep track of things

We call sections the   Atlantic
Pacific
Indian
Arctic
Antarctic

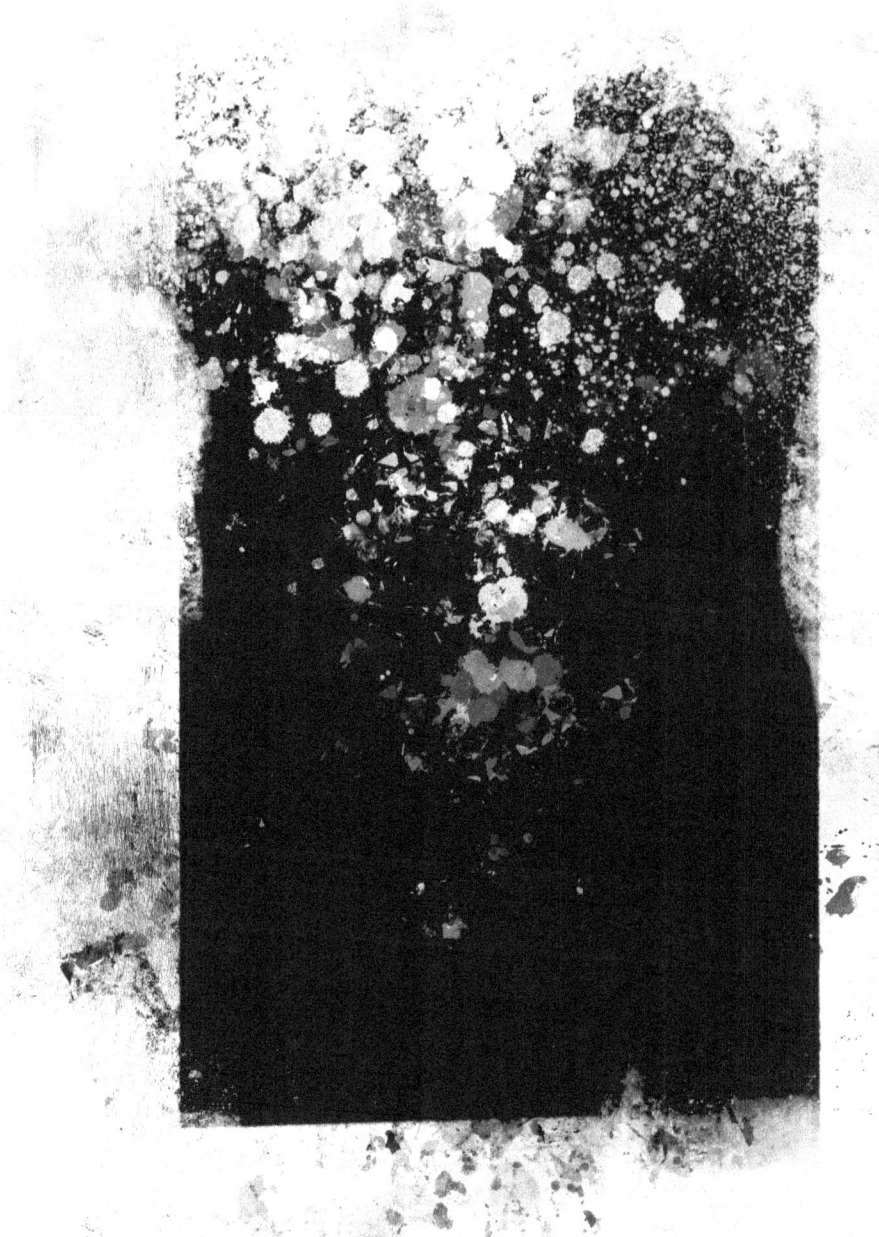

The average depth is 12,100 feet.

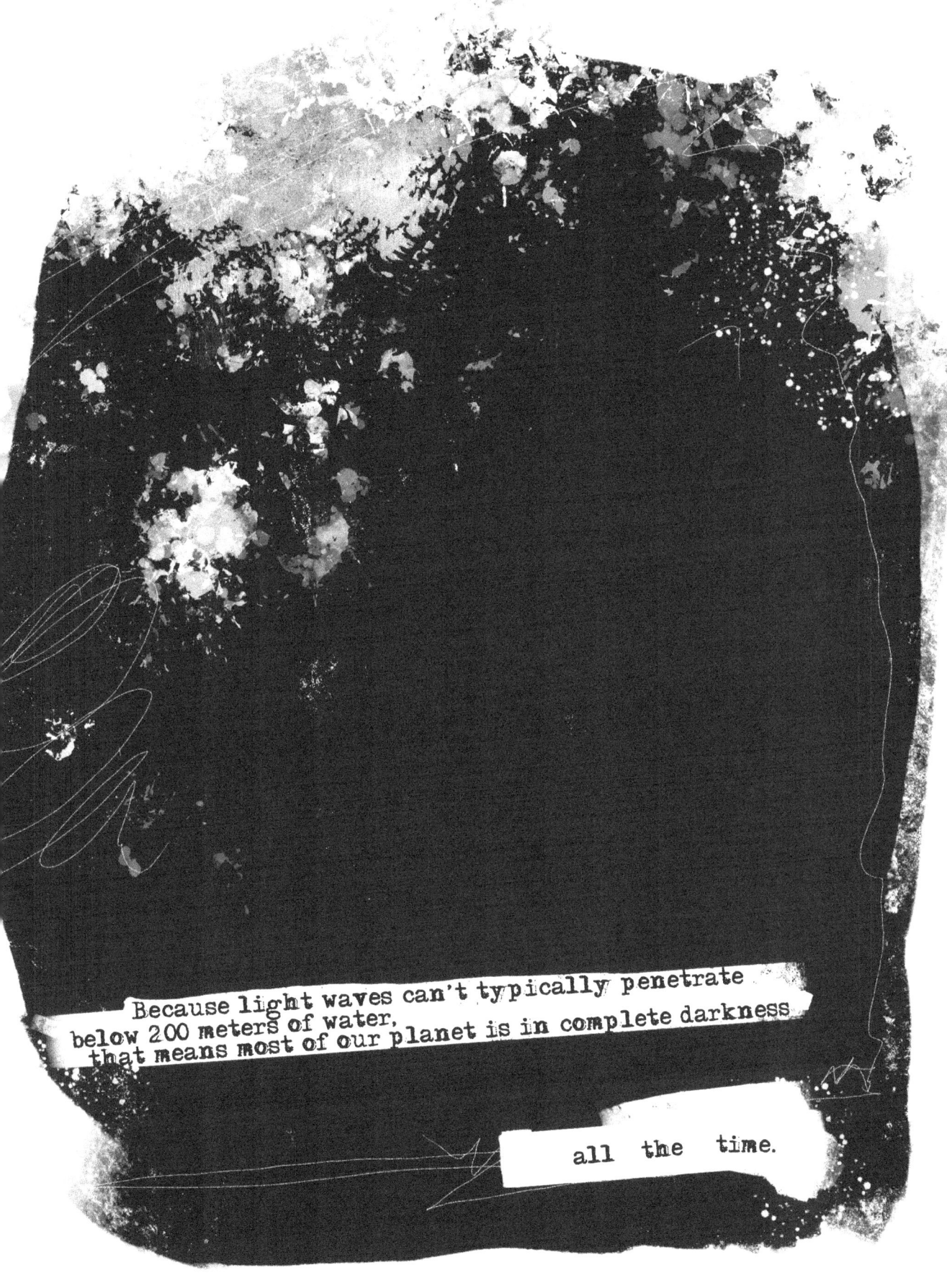

Because light waves can't typically penetrate below 200 meters of water, that means most of our planet is in complete darkness

all the time.

Wind and gravity help create the waves that we play and splash with in the shallows.

As they crash and erode the earth around us, it s incredible to know they are created by gravity and friction between the air, wind and surface water.

Waves were **not** made for a purpose or to entertain you.

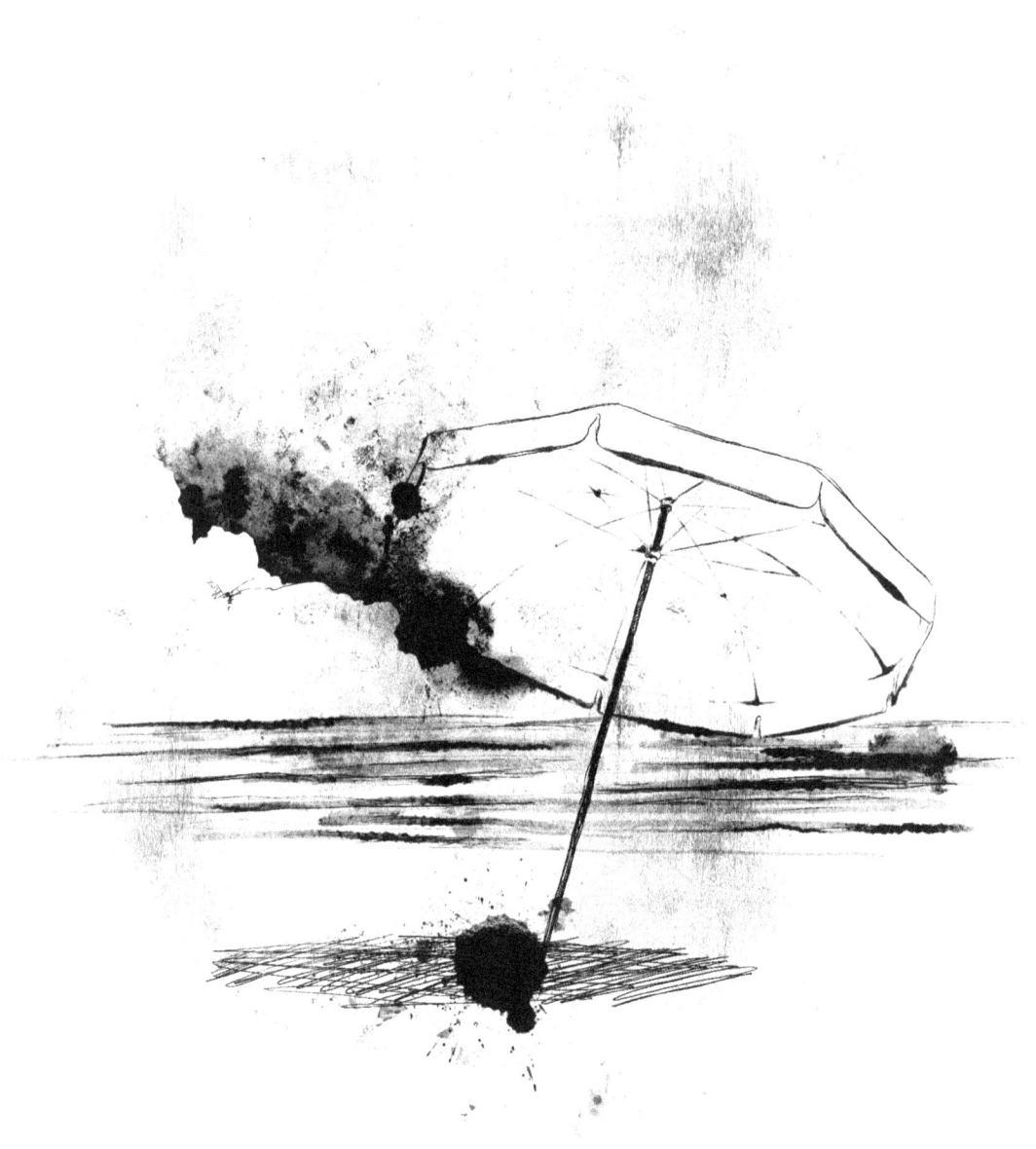

They are a product of the environment and have traveled
countless miles to wash up   on   the shore
                    and wet your   toes at
                            the beach.

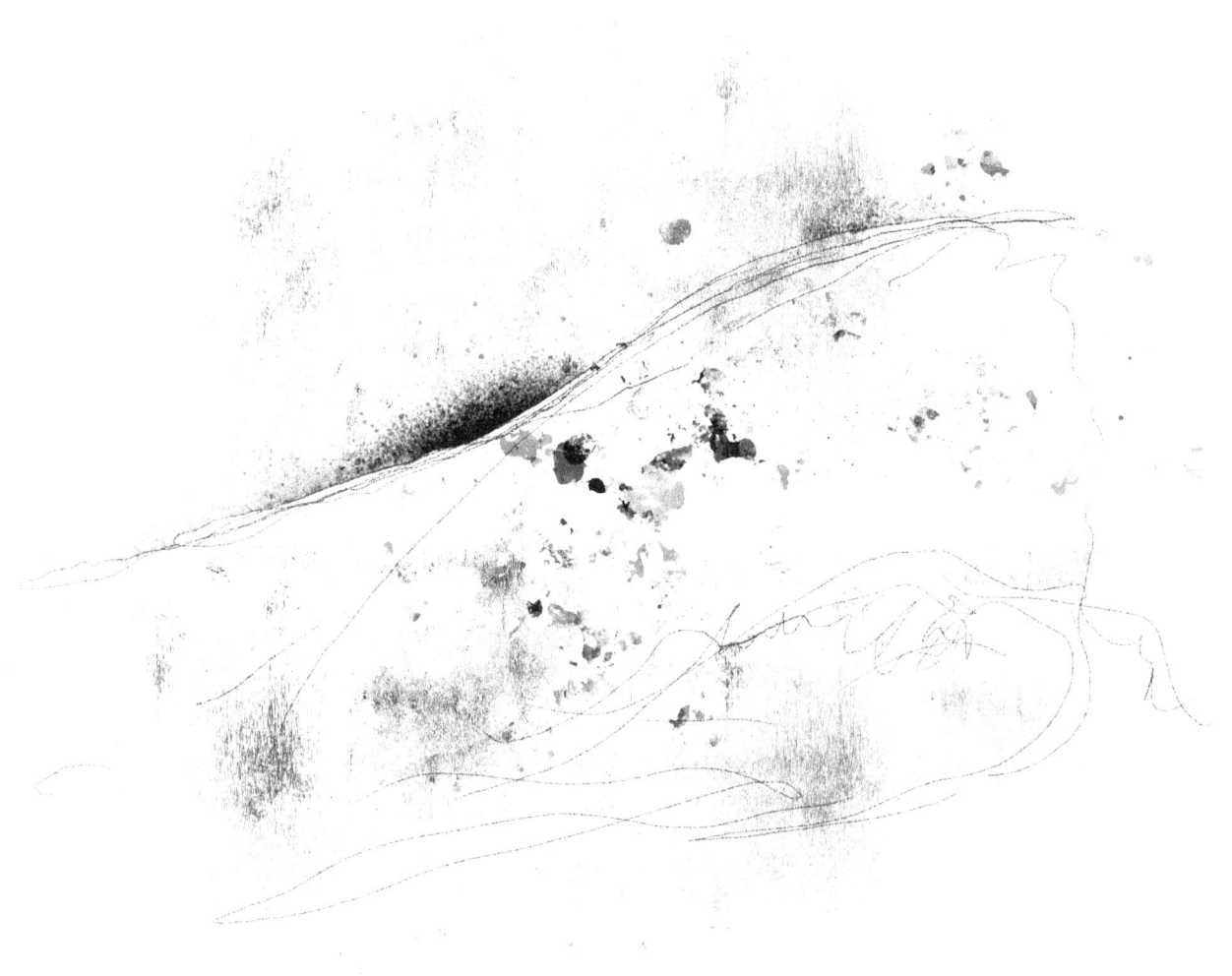

But they don t travel for you, my love.

You just happened to be

standing in the shallows.

Air is all around us.

It is made of tiny particles called   molecules

that we cannot   see.

Air creates the
  wind that moves
    your delicate hair,
      and keeps your kite
        in flight.

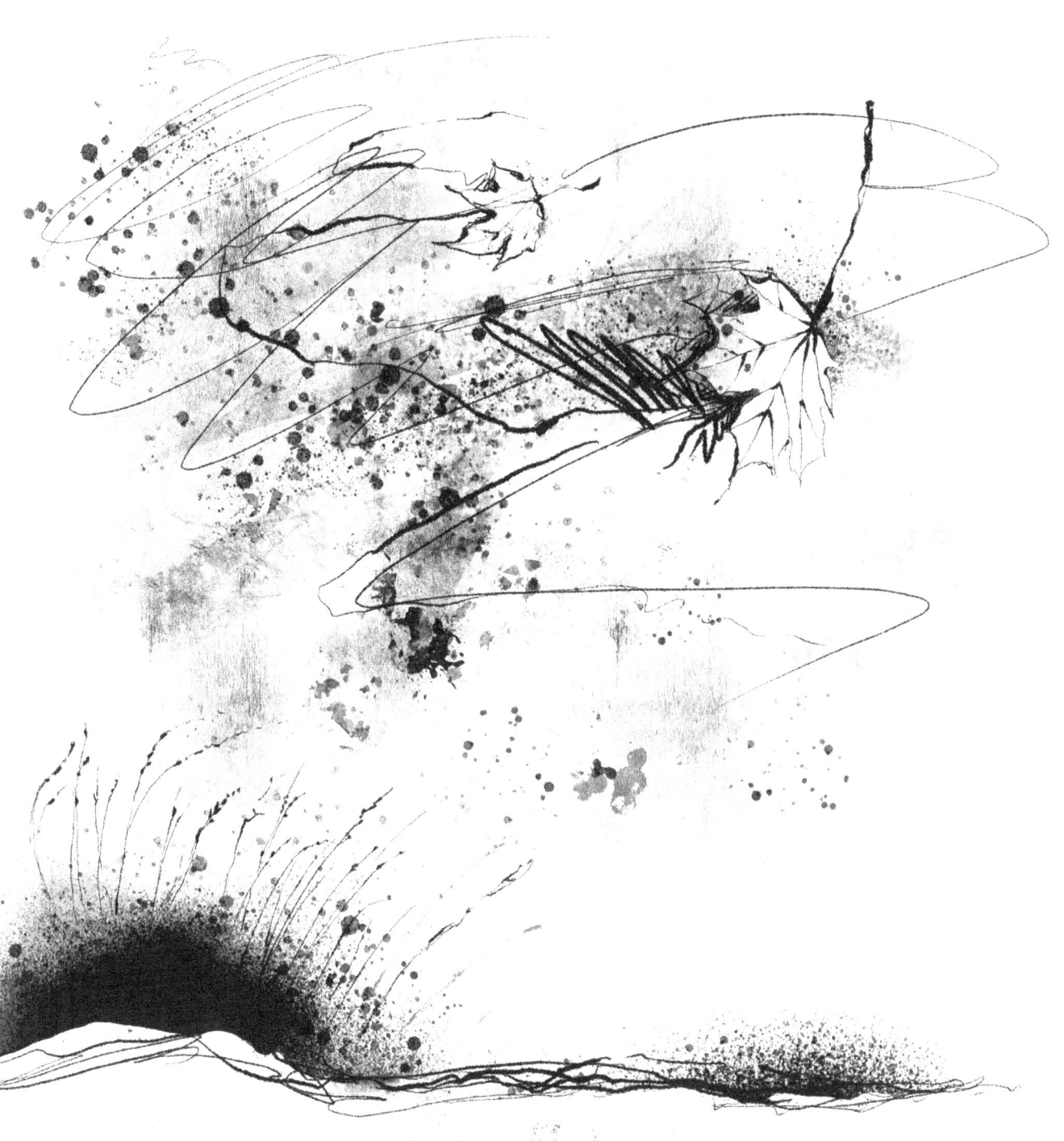

Air spins all the leaves around your head and tangles
the tall grass around your feet.

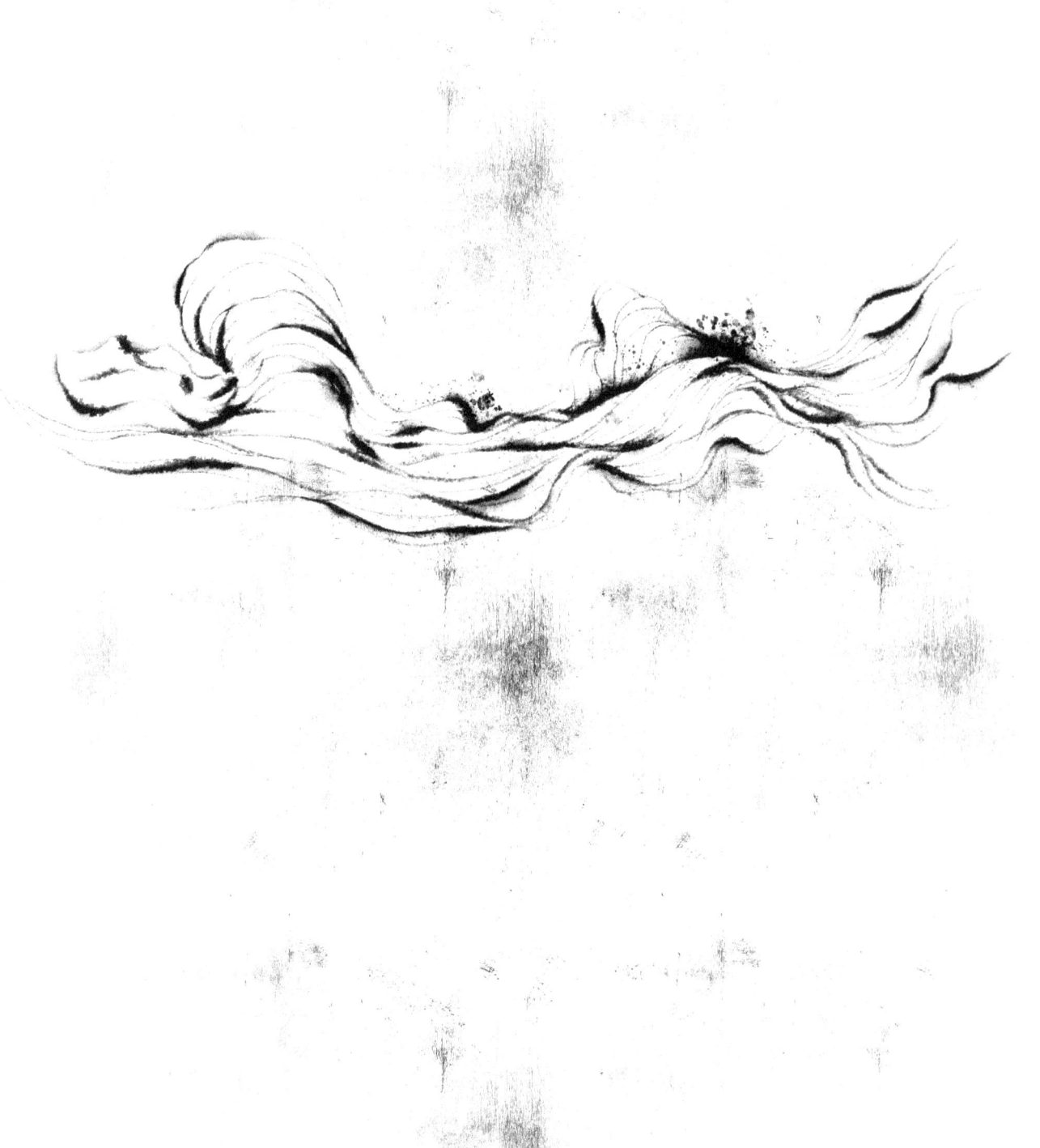

Like our mountains, ocean, and you, air has weight.

Its weight increases and

decreases with

atmosphere.

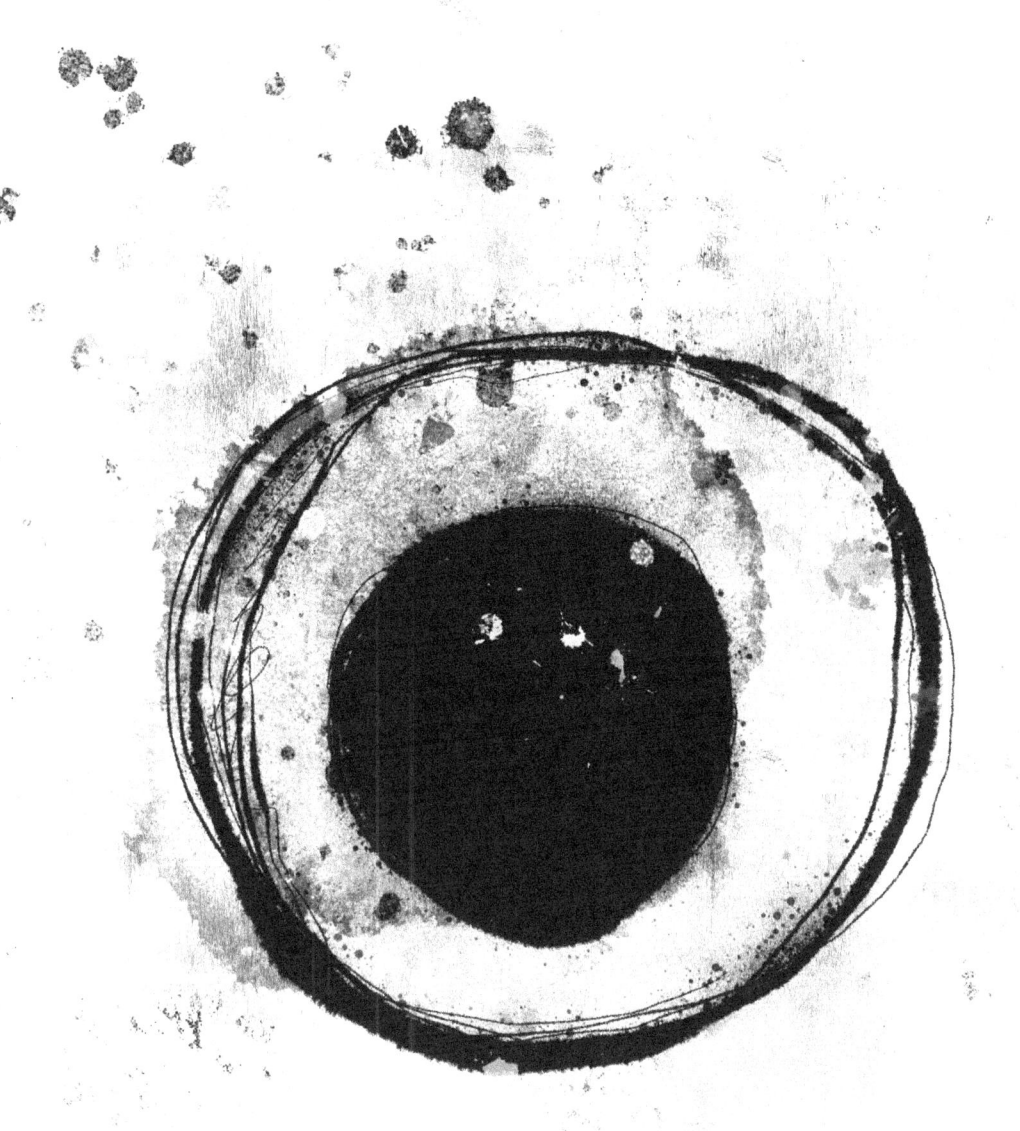

Atmosphere is what   surrounds   the Earth and,
    with the help of gravity, air
            always pushes down   on the surface below it.

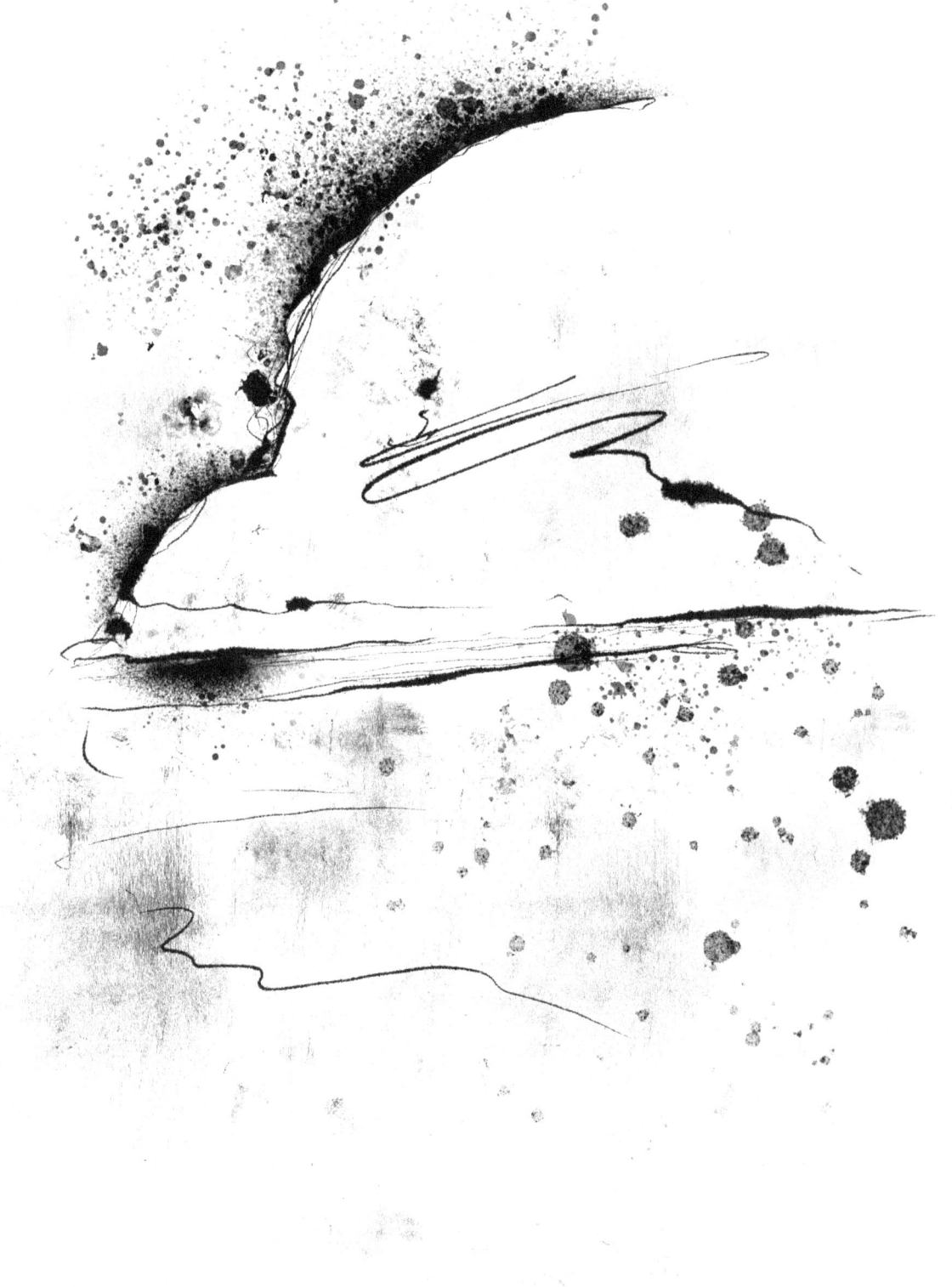

Warm winds that move mountain-size clouds
across seemingly endless   sky
                     come from air molecules.

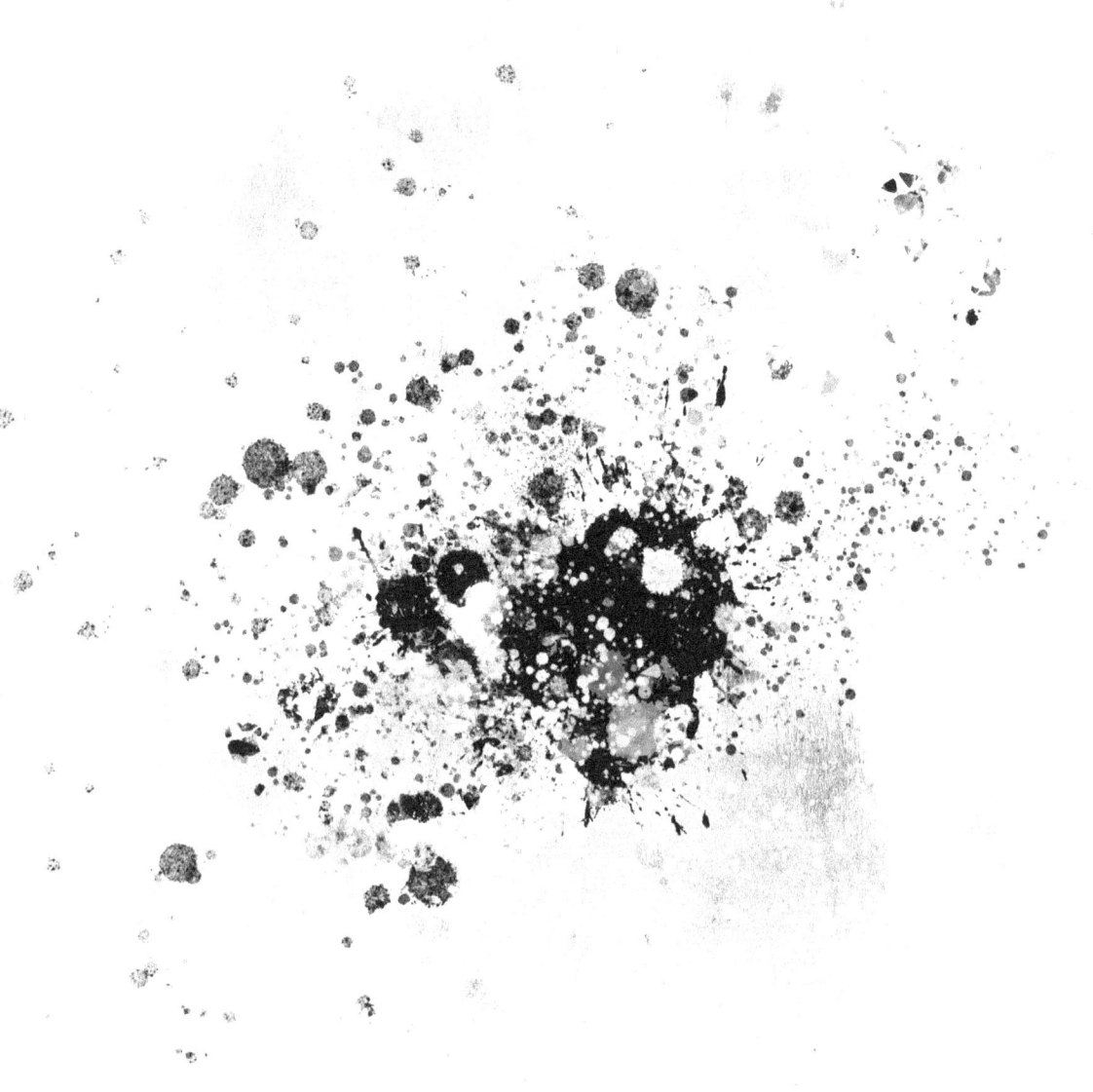

Different kinds of gasses, mostly nitrogen and oxygen, comprise air molecules.

The bigger the difference in gas pressures, the faster air will move from high to low pressure.

That rush of air is the wind we experience.

When molecules move in one direction to move your kite and
  nip at your nose,
     it's just pressure and the molecule movement that happens
                                        without you there.

                      It's not for you,

                  it's just the
                        pressure in the   air.

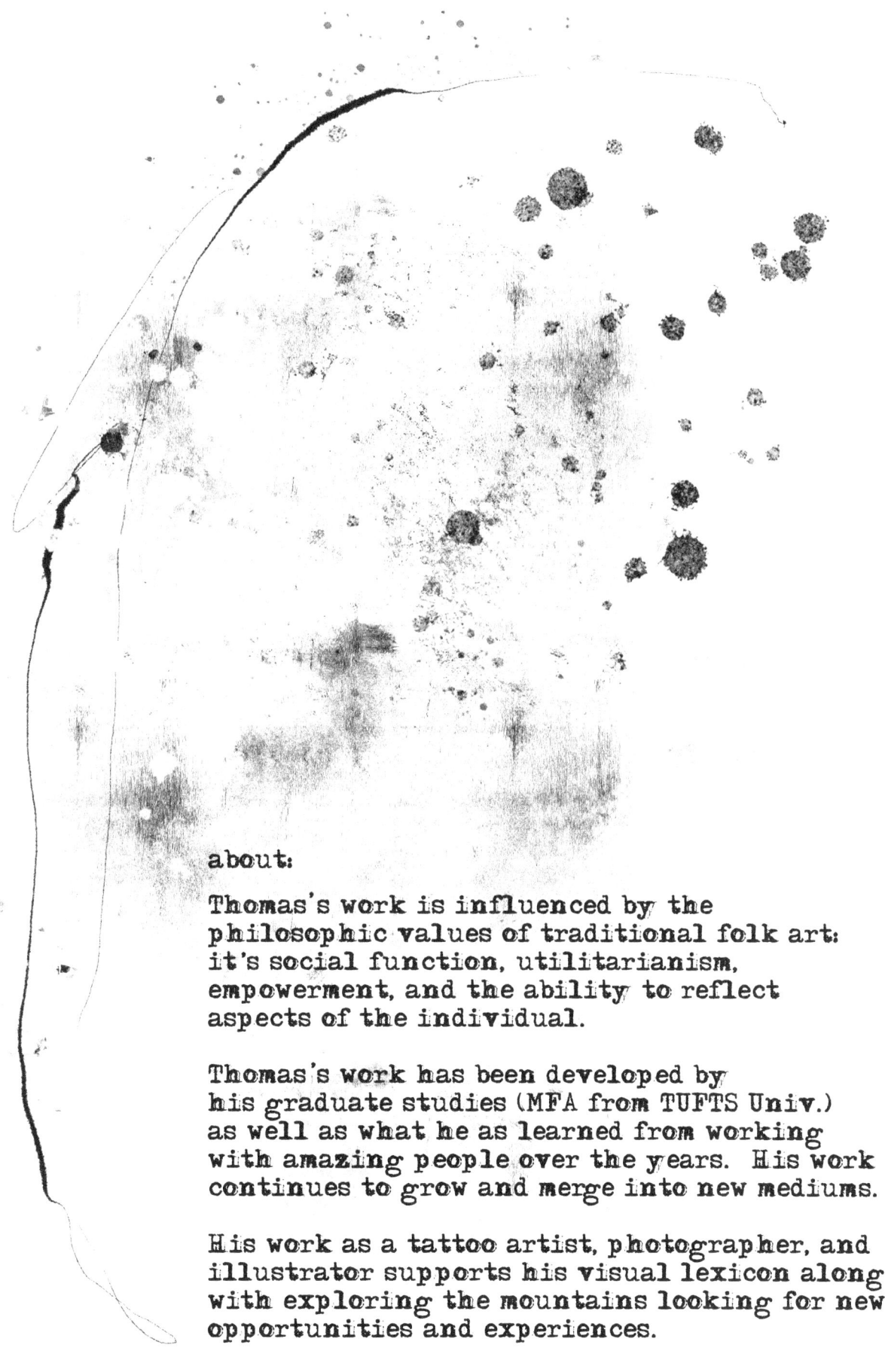

about:

Thomas's work is influenced by the philosophic values of traditional folk art: it's social function, utilitarianism, empowerment, and the ability to reflect aspects of the individual.

Thomas's work has been developed by his graduate studies (MFA from TUFTS Univ.) as well as what he as learned from working with amazing people over the years. His work continues to grow and merge into new mediums.

His work as a tattoo artist, photographer, and illustrator supports his visual lexicon along with exploring the mountains looking for new opportunities and experiences.

www.ingramcontent.com/pod-product-compliance
Lightning Source LLC
Chambersburg PA
CBHW080423190526

45161CB00004B/260